AF593511

LAWRENCE C. GOLDSMITH | A LIFE IN WATERCOLOR

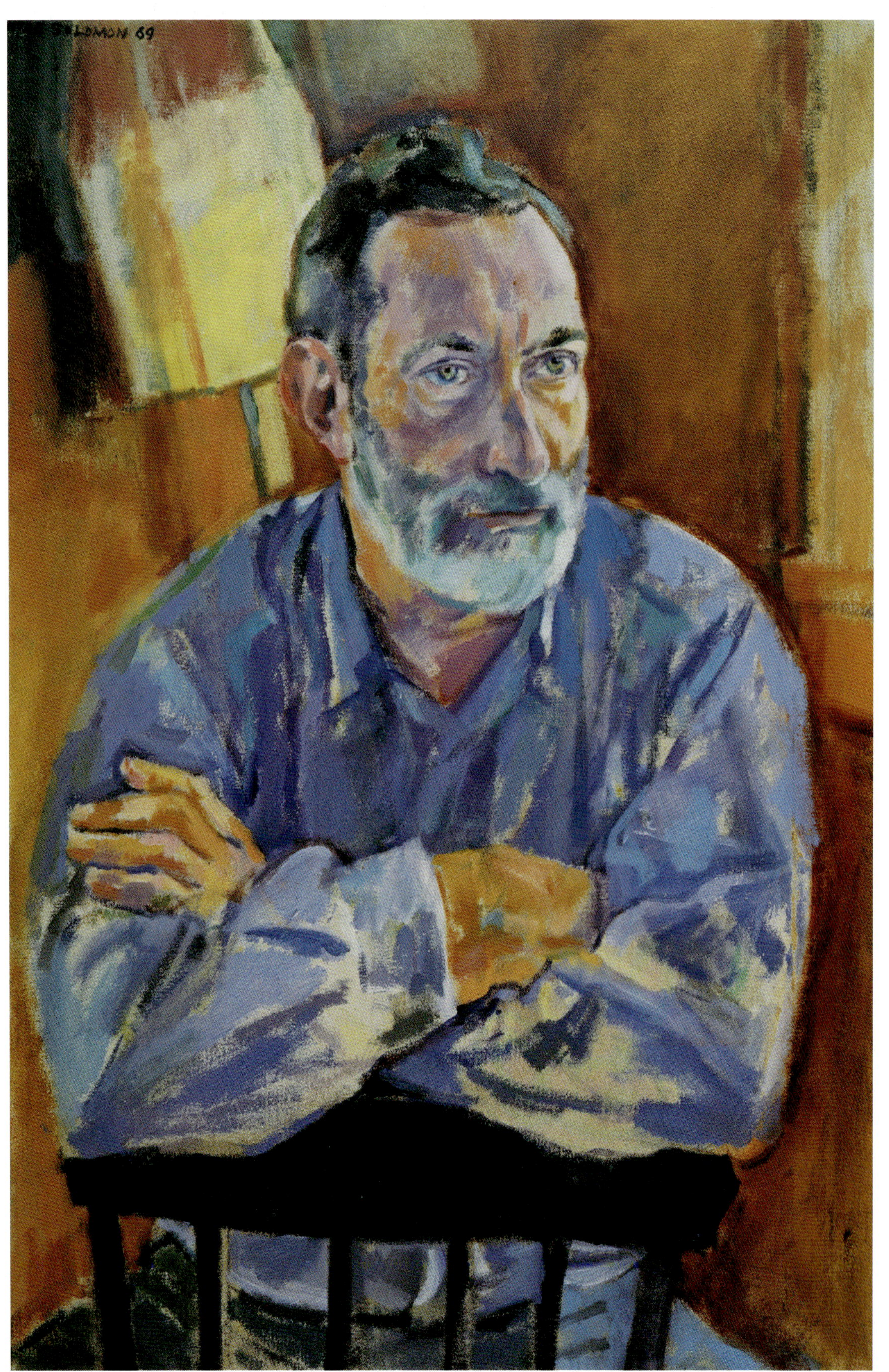

LAWRENCE C. GOLDSMITH | A LIFE IN WATERCOLOR

FOREWORD BY MEL GUSSOW

INTRODUCTION BY CARL LITTLE

HUDSON HILLS PRESS | New York and Manchester

FIRST EDITION

Published in the United States by Hudson Hills Press LLC, 74-2 Union Street, Manchester, Vermont 05254.

Distributed in the United States, its territories and possessions, and Canada by National Book Network, Inc. Distributed in the United Kingdom, Eire, and Europe by Windsor Books International.

Co-Directors: Randall Perkins and Leslie van Breen
Founding Publisher: Paul Anbinder

Editor: Margot Page
Designer: Christopher Kuntze
Proofreader: Valerie Vass
Indexer: Susan DeRenne Coerr
Color separations by Pre Tech Color, Wilder, Vermont
Printed and bound by CS Graphics Pte., Ltd., Singapore

FRONTISPIECE: *Portrait of Larry Goldsmith*, Hyde Solomon, 1969, oil on canvas, 24 x 16 inches.

LIBRARY OF CONGRESS CATALOGUING-IN-PUBLICATION DATA

Little, Carl.
Lawrence C. Goldsmith : a life in watercolor / by Carl Little. —1st ed.
p. cm.
Includes bibliographical references and index.
ISBN 1-55595-242-9 (alk. paper)
1. Goldsmith, Lawrence C., 1916—Catalogs. I. Title.
ND1839.G645A4 2004
759'.13–dc22 2003027530

CONTENTS

NOTE FROM THE PUBLISHER

The captions are the words of Larry Goldsmith.
It was his intent to offer a personal presentation of his art.

Sadly, Larry passed away on March 7, 2004, just weeks before the book went to press.

ACKNOWLEDGMENTS

As a watercolorist I have been subject to so many inspirations that it is hard to find ways of expressing sufficient gratitude to the sources. This is my opportunity to acknowledge master teachers Reuben Tam and Mario Cooper, as well as thank art historian Doris Birmingham, long-time friend and advisor; Don Holden, who can answer any question; Richard Gallen, for his wise and generous counsel; Dan Rosenblum and Richard Alther, who have boundless enthusiasm for the medium; and the loyal collectors who made this book possible.

Add to those names my beloved Lynda, who has so patiently and successfully filled the role of artist's wife. To her I dedicate this book.

L.C.G
DECEMBER 15, 2003

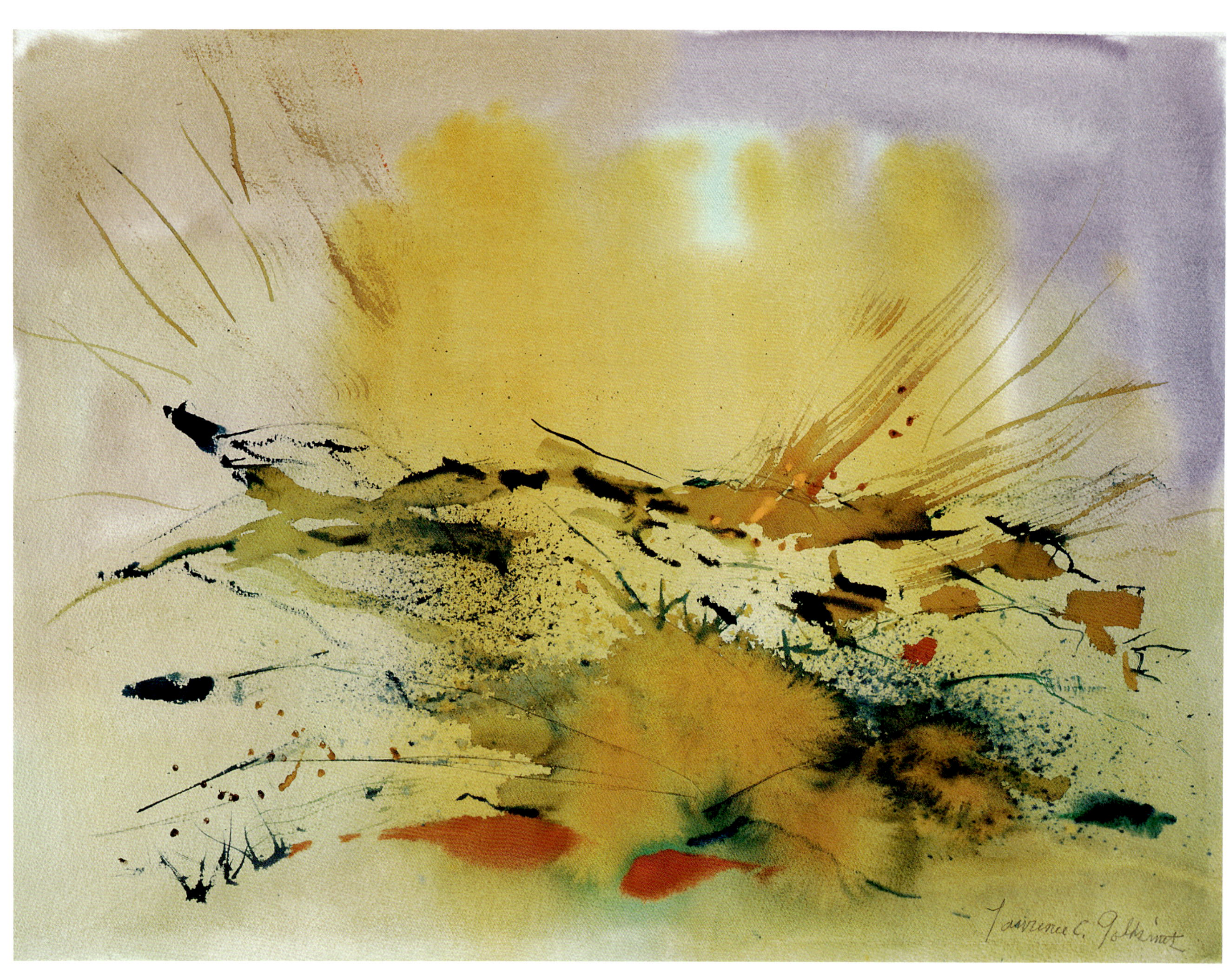

Islandia in Gold, 2002.
Utopia imagined. Dark and light colors vibrate, cast together by a golden cloud.

ISLANDIA AND LARRY GOLDSMITH

Mel Gussow

Monhegan Island, 12 miles off the coast of Maine, has been a home and a stopping place for artists since the early days of the twentieth century, when George Bellows, Winslow Homer, Robert Henri, and Rockwell Kent were stimulated by the natural environment. There is something about Monhegan that continues to inspire painters (and also sculptors and photographers). Looking back over the wide diversity of those who have worked and in many cases lived on this island, one must first note the eclecticism of the art. The range extends from those who have painstakingly recorded the daily endeavors of sailors and lobstermen in realistic detail to those who were magically transported into a world of the imagination in which nothing could specifically be identified as the island setting. There is one strong bond among the multitude of Monhegan artists—the desire to embody the landscape: the rocks and cliffs, the headlands, meadows and woods, the tidepools, the sea and the sky.

Reuben Tam was a pivotal figure in the life of Monhegan art and also in the life of Lawrence Goldsmith as artist. Tam's insight into Monhegan was verbal as well as visual; he was a poet with a brush and with words. In addition, he was the ultimate island gardener. His garden, suffused with color, was a Maine cameo of Giverny, a tradition carried on by Goldsmith. His influence on other Monhegan artists of his age and younger is as deep as it is indeterminate. Primary among those who owe a debt to him are Elena Jahn, Alan Gussow, and, of course, Goldsmith. These three—and others—mastered their individual style, but in consequent ways all must pay tribute to the purity and simplicity of Tam's vision.

Goldsmith first met Tam on Monhegan in 1963, then studied with him for a decade at the Brooklyn Museum Art School. It was from him, Goldsmith said, that his life as an artist took "a bold, new course. . . . I was inspired by this watercolor pioneer who painted landscapes and seascapes in a semi-abstract style. Reuben Tam had dared depart from the conventional realism that has imprisoned so much of watercolor painting for so long (and still does)."

For many years Goldsmith painted outdoors, an artist on location; in recent years he has worked in his studio drawing on his memories. For him, as for others, Monhegan has remained a fountain of youthful exuberance. Influenced by Turner and the French Impressionists, he paints with a kind of controlled abandon. With broad but delicate brushstrokes, he captures the immediacy of the swiftly changing landscape, how a sudden shift in the sun or the tide can alter the scenic wonderment. At the same time, there is a feeling of permanence. The beauty will hold, fixed in time by the artist's perception. The placidity of the painting titled *Becalmed,* 2001 (Plate 49), a sea at rest, can suddenly, with a dash of wave, seem to have dark undercurrents as in *Where the Sea Begins,* 2000 (Plate 48). Something similar occurs when Goldsmith paints the Vermont mountains, but it is the island setting that most concerns me.

Monhegan has brought me closer to art and to its artists, to those mentioned above and also to Zero Mostel, who, walking down to meet the mailboat, would rather talk about art than about theater; to Arline Simon, James Wyeth, and to the others who have found inspiration in the endlessly beautiful place that Goldsmith calls Islandia, "an artist's paradise."

LAWRENCE GOLDSMITH | PASSION OF PLACE

Carl Little

TO REACH the island of Monhegan, Maine, I take the *Laura B* from Port Clyde, a distance of twelve or so miles. On the trip over, I scan the sea for harbor porpoise and seals, a common sight in these waters. As the island and its remarkable companion, Manana, begin to rise out of the water, I recall the words of an early travel writer: "the sleeping whales that lie warming their huge backs in the sun."[1]

Lawrence Goldsmith has spent 40 summers on the island of Monhegan and twenty years, with his wife Lynda, a botanist specializing in begonias, in a gray-shingled house perched on a ledge overlooking the Atlantic. From their deck, the coast of Maine and Boothbay Harbor are a faint outline on the horizon. While Goldsmith has painted in other parts of the world—the Caribbean, Mexico, South America, Canada, Arizona, California and Florida, among other places—this Maine island and his winter home in Fairfax, Vermont, have nurtured his love of nature for much of his life as a mature artist.

Now in his mid-eighties, Lawrence Goldsmith has been painting for much of his life. He can easily take you back to his childhood when he was encouraged to pursue "advantages;" recognizing his skill in drawing, his mother thought he might one day be an architect. Goldsmith would take a few stabs in that direction, but a different creative passion would win over his heart and hand: painting.

The future artist was born in New York City in 1916 and grew up in Scarsdale, in Westchester County. His family numbered six: himself, his mother and stepfather, a sister and two half-sisters (his father died when he was a year and a half old). A somewhat shy boy with little interest in competitive sports, Larry found he was most comfortable exploring nature (he attended summer camps in Maine). His love of the natural world would carry over into the land- and seascapes that number among his greatest works of art.

Goldsmith's first real training as an artist came early. Around the age of ten or eleven, he was sent to the Grand Central School of Art for lessons. He was, he recalls, the youngest student there. Located in Grand Central Station in the heart of Manhattan, the school was run by Edmund Greacen, whose Impressionist canvases struck the young Goldsmith as quite extraordinary—perhaps his first encounter with modern art (as he lived "in the country," he rarely visited museums or galleries as a youngster). He took lessons with Greacen's daughter, Nan, drawing from the cast.

Goldsmith attended Yale University, graduating in 1939. While there, he took studio courses at the Yale School of Fine Arts. At the time, the school was, in the painter's estimation, “good but complacent,” not the dynamic place it would become when Josef Albers took over as director. The painter remembers spending six weeks drawing one cube and then another six weeks drawing a cube on top of a cube. Studies of Grecian heads followed.

If his courses at Yale were rather dreary, Goldsmith found a more engaging instructor outside the university, the master watercolorist Eliot O’Hara. O’Hara was renowned as one of the most competent and energetic teachers of watercolor; some of his books on the medium are still in print. Goldsmith learned a great deal from him and he credits O’Hara with inspiring a life-long interest in watercolor.

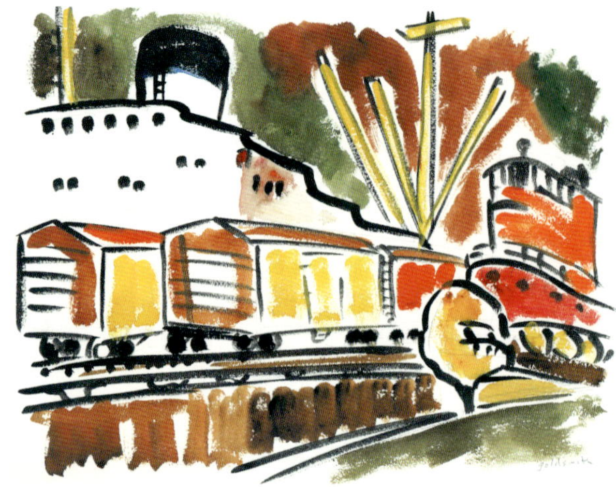

Fulton Fish Market New York, 1940. 12¼ x 16 in.

After graduating from Yale and returning to New York, the young artist took courses each year to continue his education. He remembers classes with Will Barnet and Philip Evergood. He also audited Meyer Shapiro’s lectures at the New School for Social Research. These slide talks, which revolved around Cézanne and the Impressionists, helped Goldsmith better understand modern art while adding focus to his aesthetic considerations.

During World War II, Goldsmith worked in the Office of War Information in New York, writing news broadcasts aimed at Europe by short-wave radio. He had hoped to serve in the military but he was turned down because he was classified 4F for medical reasons by the draft board, making him ineligible to serve.

While earning a living doing editorial work for various publications (including *Medical Economics*, *Family Circle,* and the *New York Herald Tribune Sunday Magazine*), Goldsmith continued to paint, devoting weekends and vacations to practicing watercolor and other mediums. He remembers painting excursions along the Hudson River with John Bailey, the humor editor at the *Saturday Evening Post*, and Frank Modell, a *New Yorker* cartoonist. When he was in college, he went on several trips to Europe with his childhood friend, the painter Carl Hiller. He also painted along the seashore on Fire Island and in lower Manhattan, in the area that is now the South Street Seaport.

Becoming more serious about his commitment as a painter, he enrolled at the Art Students League. For a dozen or so years, he took classes at the league. It was under the tutelage of Mario Cooper that Goldsmith gained further skill in watercolor. The artist, who was president of the American Watercolor Society, was a master technician.[2] He practiced a representational style, his watercolors tight and controlled. On several occasions, Goldsmith would fill in for Cooper when the instructor couldn’t make a class.

While this training gained him confidence and skill, Goldsmith had yet to discover himself as a painter. It took a trip to an island off the coast of Maine and a visit with an American master to set him firmly on his course.

Many serious and famous artists spend their summers on the island [Monhegan]. It's a good place to work, not only because of its beauty but also because of the general atmosphere of quiet purpose.

Louise Dickinson Rich, *The Coast of Maine* (1975)[3]

GOLDSMITH first heard about Monhegan Island in the early 1960s. A friend described the rugged, rocky, windswept island and discouraged the painter from going there, saying it would be difficult to circumnavigate. Later, at a party hosted by Henry Kallem, an artist who frequented Monhegan, Goldsmith saw for the first time—by way of 3-D slides—the actual place. He liked the looks of the island and decided to make the trip.

Monhegan has been drawing artists to its formidable and somewhat forbidding shores for well over one hundred years. From Hudson River School painters to artists from the Ashcan School, from realists to impressionists and modernists, men and women have sought a refuge, a loose-knit art colony and, as Maine writer Rich simply put it, "a good place to work."

The painter George Bellows, upon his first visit to the island in July 1911, provided some of the most direct testimony as to Monhegan's magnificence. "This is the most wonderful country ever modeled by the hand of the master architect," he wrote his wife, Emma. "The island is only a mile wide and two miles long, but it looks as large as the Rocky Mountains."[4] Whatever its precise measurements, Bellows captured the impression of grandeur Monhegan imparts on everyone who spends time there.

Goldsmith made his first trip to what he calls an "artist's paradise" in 1964. He saw for himself the mighty headlands, the mysterious Cathedral Woods that lie at the heart of the island, and the numerous coves, ledges, and other landmarks that mark the shoreline, from the Washerwoman to Pulpit Rock. If you ask him what his favorite spot is, he may tell you Squeaker Cove, a dramatic indentation between White and Black Head on the eastern shore, but he may also suggest you "go anywhere."

As is the case today, artists at that time opened their studios to visitors several days a week, inviting them to view and maybe purchase a work. When Goldsmith stepped into Reuben Tam's island atelier, he encountered a room full of semi-abstract landscapes, evocations of weather and islands and rock. Overwhelmed by the art, he remembers saying to himself, "That's the way I would like to paint."

The Hawaiian-born Tam (1916–1994) had first arrived at Monhegan in 1948 and spent every subsequent summer on the island (he returned to his native Kauai in 1980, never to return to Maine). In a statement printed in the landmark survey *Art USA Now*, published in 1963, he described his aesthetic approach: "I paint to embody the spirit of place and thus make objective those poetic conditions, portents, and possibilities of nature that move me deeply and hauntingly."[5] His new admirer, Lawrence Goldsmith, would soon embrace and emulate this perspective.

Goldsmith arranged to study with Tam when he returned to New York. Tam taught color, composition, and other basics of painting at the Brooklyn Museum Art School, combining technical instruction with informal lectures on art history and the contemporary art world (he made regular rounds of the New York galleries and museums). Tam's openness to a wide range of aesthetics left an indelible impression on his protege.

When he speaks of his teacher's particular strengths as an artist, Goldsmith might be speaking about himself. "Tam had this wonderful sensitivity to color and line and shape," he told an interviewer in 1993, "and he was able to grasp the integrity and beauty of a scene in nature without going into an abundance of detail." Goldsmith admired the way Tam could capture the scene with a few gestures in pen and ink or acrylic or oil, leaving out all the non-essentials.

Tam was one of a group of "advanced" painters who had discovered Monhegan.[6] Hyde Solomon, John Hultberg, Hans Moller, Charles Martin, Joseph DeMartini, Glen Krause, William and Jan McCartin, Michael Loew, Alexander Minewski, William Manning—these and other painters responded to the island by way of abstract means, representing their surroundings without replicating them. While many of them, like Goldsmith, pursued other livelihoods that supported them, they were one and all committed to a serious pursuit of personal vision.

Goldsmith studied with Tam for about six years. While he felt he could have gone on taking classes with him, Goldsmith finally felt it was time to strike out on his own, to work independently. He would aspire to Tam's aesthetic philosophy while exploring a distinct watercolor vision.

"To paint good watercolors is a full-time job, not a relaxation from other kinds of artistic expression...."

Eliot O'Hara, *Making Watercolor Behave* (1923)[7]

Watercolor has a reputation for being unruly, as underscored by the title of Eliot O'Hara's book. At the time Goldsmith was studying with the master watercolorist in New Haven, he probably wanted to know how to make the fluid medium respond to his hand. Over time and under the influence of Reuben Tam, however, he became bolder and freer with the flowing medium.

While he has consistently painted in oil and acrylic over the years, Goldsmith's greatest accomplishments as an artist have come in the medium of watercolor. From the earliest work—a dynamic study of Washington Square Park pigeons, *City Dwellers,* 1960 (Plate 1)—to the most recent—an abstract Monhegan piece titled *From Jamie's Bench* (Plate 6)[8] painted in 2002—his sure hand and poetic eye are on display.

Elsewhere in *Making Watercolor Behave*, O'Hara stated that watercolors should not be literal. "A lone figure plodding his way home won't do any more," he wrote. "What you suggest," he stated, "should be not what some individual may be going to do or has done, but what the beholder would feel about the place if he were on that road . . . ."[9] Or, Goldsmith might add, "that island."

Whether or not he first heard these or similar words of wisdom from O'Hara himself, Goldsmith practices this approach. "I try to paint. . . not what [the landscape] looks like but what it feels like," the painter explains. "What I'm after is the person looking at the painting responding in his or her own emotional way to what I've seen of the subject."

Goldsmith combines the formal values of abstraction with a romantic identification with nature. Imagination and inventiveness lead to spirited paintings and watercolor serves to develop the mood quickly and definitely.

Goldsmith's watercolors can not be defined as realistic. While you may easily recognize a motif, as in a rendering of a Mexican fireworks display or a study of mangrove roots in Florida (both watercolors dated 1972, see Plates 7 and 8), even these more representational pieces are not full of details, but rather evoke their subjects. As the artist notes, apropos of his Monhegan paintings, one cannot look at any island watercolor and say, "Oh, Goldsmith must have been sitting on Sherm Stanley's porch when he did that one."

You need to be a bold watercolorist to paint Monhegan Island. For many years,

Goldsmith was one of the few full-time summer painters who worked *en plein air*, perched on a rocky outcropping, a sheet of watercolor taped to a stiff surface, his paints and brushes at either side. Precautions were necessary, for one could experience weather extremes in a single day, going from intense sunlight, which can dry the watercolor too quickly, to thick fog, which can make it too wet. In recent years, Goldsmith has worked in his studio with a work table on rollers that allows him to capture the light as it streams through skylights.

An assortment of techniques adds dynamism and atmosphere to Goldsmith's work. Spattering and a variety of linework produce different effects; he also consistently contrasts broad washes with linear accents. A spruce twig stripped of needles may be used to create a "nervous" personal line that energizes the painting. Twisted pieces of Kleenex often serve to create an outline that is almost kinetic and diametrically opposed to something made by mechanical brushwork. Other unusual tools include a dental pick and the edge of a cut-up credit card, which make distinctive marks.

While he often uses rough 140-weight Arches paper, Goldsmith prefers the English-made Whatman stock. "Whatman has a rare ability to work dry-brush on a glittering white surface," the artist explains. He takes advantage of these qualities in such paintings as *Blue Spot,* 1999 (Plate 60). "It's such a beautiful paper," he remarks with a smile, "it's a shame to put color on it."

Part of Monhegan's appeal to artists lies in its atmosphere, an elemental mix of sky, sea, fog, rocks, and trees. It can have a mysterious quality to it, a kind of *Ultima Thule* in the Gulf of Maine. Inspired by this sense of mystery, Goldsmith borrowed *Islandia,* the title of Austin Tappan Wright's classic novel, for the titles of some of his island landscapes.[10]

Goldsmith believes in taking liberties with a subject, seeking to get away from reality as it is conventionally expressed. Thus, in a painting titled *White Caps,* 1998 (Plate 46), he uses his own forms and contrasts to express the turbulence of wave tops. "They are more felt than seen," he notes, which lends them greater strength. Another painting, *Blast!,* 1988 (Plate 50), conjures up the turbulent sea without resorting to histrionics.

In the long line of Monhegan painters, the island's headlands have been a favorite subject. Here again, Goldsmith's treatment of a well-known motif tends to be out of the ordinary. In *Lonely Headlands,* 1986 (Plate 37), for example, the light haze symbolizes infinity as an expression of solitude.

The island's rocks also undergo transformation. Goldsmith plays fast and loose with this well-known island subject in a number of works, including *Rocky Command,* 1998 (Plate 31), and *So Many Rocks,* 1997 (Plate 29).[11] He notes that the island was once a mountain peak—"a bold monadnock," Rachel Carson called it in *The Edge of the Sea* (1955).[12]

One of the few vertical pieces in the book, *Solo,* 1964 (Plate 24), is a monochromatic painting inspired by a "lordly" dead fir tree on Monhegan. You can almost sense the life of this tree that has endured many Maine winters. In another arboreal fantasy, *Twig Light,* 1996 (Plate 20), painted in Vermont, white lines scratched in with a dental pick add luster to what would otherwise be a dark and light woods scene. As is the case elsewhere, the activated surface is of greater importance than the sense of depth.

Goldsmith's watercolors are a wonderful mix of emotion, movement, and color excitement. In a painting like *Torrid Memories,* 1989 (Plate 9), he creates mood through bursts of oranges and subdued grays. Warm colors, a quiet gentleness, and a certain timelessness are other common qualities of these watercolors.

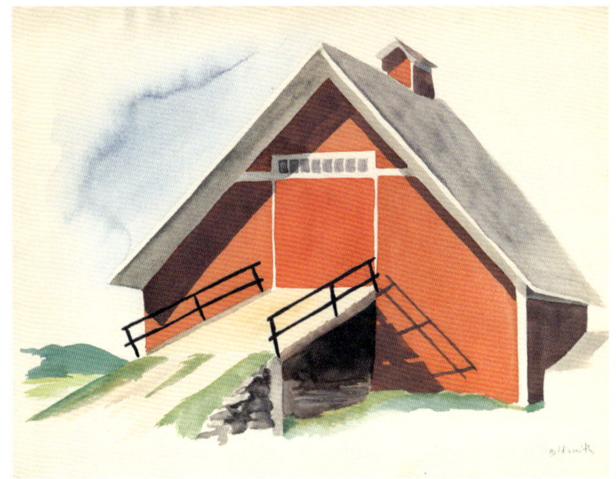
Vermont Barn, 1949. 14½ x 19 in.

Fairfax, Vermont, is Goldsmith's other place for painting. During World War II, he was writing freelance and rented a summer cottage on Lake Champlain. When the war let up and gas rationing lessened, he was able to drive through the Vermont countryside where he found a beautiful old brick farmhouse, which he eventually purchased, along with 38 acres of land, in 1946. The house, with its 24-inch-wide plank floors, required extensive repairs; at the time of the purchase, the house had only two standing brick walls and there were 34 missing windows.

The house overlooks the Lamoille River and, beyond, Mount Mansfield. When Goldsmith determined that he wanted to be a landscape painter, it seemed logical to move to Vermont from Greenwich Village. The brick house became a permanent home. He eventually added on a serviceable studio, about 38 by 30 feet, with a woodstove and no water pipes (he did not want to risk frozen pipes). The studio was designed for north light.

The painter employs a wide palette related to his subject matter. In the lively Vermont piece *Green Lands,* 2002 (Plate 22), he embraces a color many watercolorists steer clear of. "Watercolor provides a vast variety of greens," he notes. In mixing his colors, he makes a new green every time.

After a hike up Mount Mansfield, the highest peak in Vermont, Goldsmith was inspired to paint *Mountaintop Outlook,* 1978 (Plate 15), a "lateral" view that evokes the sweep of distance. In presenting this abstracted vista, he invites his viewer to imagine his own widest views.

Goldsmith is an all-season painter. His images of Vermont winter capture the inherent color of the landscape. In *Winter Light in Vermont,* 1973 (Plate 13), he intensifies what he calls the "slight color" of the season to subtle effect. A painting like *Snow,* 1999 (Plate 21), stimulates the emotions we feel when confronted with a snowfall. Writing about another winter piece, *Snowflakes,* 1979 (Plate 16), Goldsmith voices an age-old sentiment: "For all its beauty, nature vies with the human spirit again and again."

Some of Goldsmith's Monhegan watercolors were painted in Vermont. "I can dream of the summers," he related in a recent interview, "and still do a version of Lobster Cove or Seal Ledges." Memories can be as intense as actually standing in front of the motif. Goldsmith once thought to use photographs as *aides memoire*, but he abandoned that idea. In fact, his own watercolors may inspire other paintings—like variations on a theme.

Indeed, Goldsmith frequently works in series. In a group of watercolors titled *North by Northeast,* he evokes New England horizons and the openness of the landscape. Color is intensified and watercolor washes are mostly transparent. Another series, *Travelogue,* conjures up different parts of the world using horizontal bars of color, with the merest suggestion of sky and horizon. A third series, *Oriental Legends,* Goldsmith has described as "unconscious reflections" of his visits to Hong Kong, Bali, Java, and Sri Lanka.

Goldsmith speaks knowingly of the pitfalls of his chosen medium and of the difficulty some artists have deciding when a picture is finished. While some watercolorists are known to work for extended amounts of time on a painting, his own experience and instincts teach him not to belabor the process for fear of over-painting, of losing the wonderful fluidity and transparency that are watercolor's special qualities. "The painting is done when it achieves a balance," he states, "by way of the weights and counterweights of color and movement."

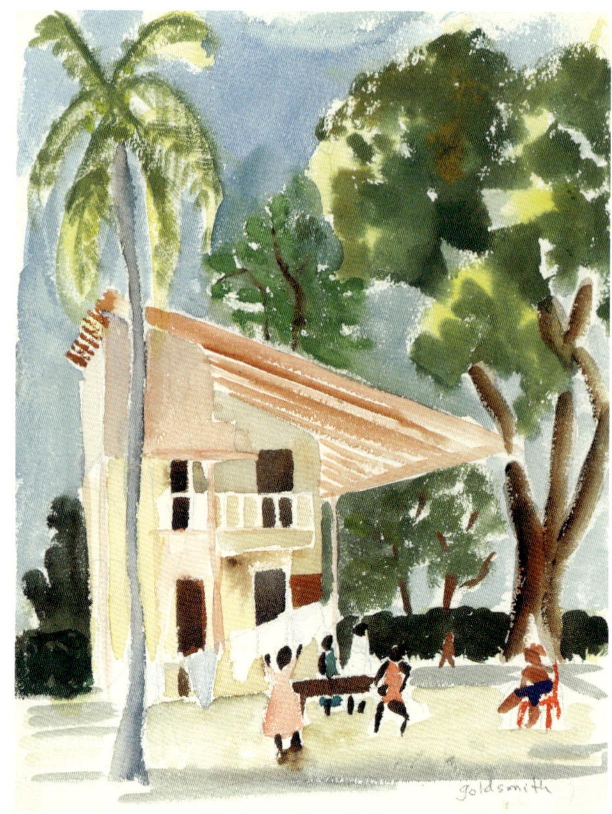

Haitian Villagers, 1952. 12 x 9 in.

When asked how long a watercolor takes to create, Goldsmith describes what is often a three-day process. He thinks about the subject the first day, dreaming about what it will be; on the second day, he does the actual painting; and on the third day he contemplates the work, perhaps adding a little touch here and there. He paraphrases an old saying: "You have to do a mile of good watercolors before there's one you're satisfied with."

Over time, especially in the past fifteen or so years, Goldsmith has sought to become more abstract in his work. In an article about his work that appeared in the magazine *Watercolor 92*, the artist offered this bit of alliterative advice: "Let the paint paint the painting."[13] Where he was more deliberative in his early years (he sometimes sketched in a basic outline for the watercolor), in more recent times he has just let things happen.

In a film made by his cinematographer son Paul, *Bold and Free: The Watercolor Techniques of Lawrence C. Goldsmith* (1997), the artist is shown tilting the sheets of paper to encourage the paint to flow even more than it normally does. Being that free in letting things develop means that images that Goldsmith never would have imagined happen on the paper. It's a virtuoso performance, liberating in its appeal.

"I take chances and invite the risk of wasting time and paper," Goldsmith admits. Yet by going with the flow of his favored medium, the painter avers, "I sometimes get a real reward."

"Our medium can do things no other medium can."

Lawrence Goldsmith, *Watercolor Bold & Free*[14]

When asked about his influences, Goldsmith will often start with his teacher Reuben Tam. He also looks back to J.M.W. Turner's watercolor sketches, John Marin's dynamic, semi-abstract aquarelles, and Paul Jenkins' fluid inventions. Some of his works pay homage to the color field paintings of Mark Rothko; others recall the tone poems of Whistler or the atmospheric landscapes of the Oriental masters.

While he admires the watercolors of Winslow Homer and Andrew Wyeth, Goldsmith has never been attracted to their style of realism. It is not a matter of being cerebral; he simply strives for something very different in his work: spiritual moods, the beauty of reflection, and inner privacy.

In his landmark *Watercolor Bold & Free*, published in 1980, Goldsmith celebrates the more abstract realms of watercolor. "What watercolor offers—as does no other medium—, " Goldsmith writes, "is the unique interplay of the quick dissolution of pigment in water spreading over sparkling white watercolor paper." Alluding to the beauty of the accidental, of the need to loosen up, he cites John Marin: "Painting is founded on the heart controlled by the hand."

Goldsmith also cautions that when a painter broaches new territory that is less realistic, he or she "may be in for a hard time" with their "closest admirers." Freedom has its costs; "disappointments," he notes, "are inevitable." Yet Goldsmith remains optimistic and encouraging. "Experimentation is priceless," he avows, and he reassures new artists that their "feelings *and* abilities will ultimately coincide."

The painter knows whereof he speaks. Over time, his feelings and skills as a watercolorist have converged, resulting in paintings that have gained him a goodly amount of acclaim. A Signature member of the American Watercolor Society, Goldsmith has exhibited in numerous solo and group shows over the years, is represented in many prestigious museums and private collections, and has had his art reproduced in more than a dozen books.

Goldsmith has also passed on his knowledge to numerous students through courses taught at Queens College, the Jackson Heights, New York, Arts Club, and the University of Vermont's Church Street Center. He has conducted watercolor workshops across the United States and in Canada, from Monhegan to Loma Linda University in Riverside, California, from Scottsdale, Arizona, to Vankleek Hill in Ontario. He still has a loyal group of artists who work with him in his Vermont studio.

In the early 1990s Goldsmith realized he had macular degeneration, a common and unfortunate ailment that eventually leads to blindness. In the year 2000 the condition worsened; he felt like he was in the midst of a Monhegan fog.

Although he does not see colors or shapes clearly, Goldsmith refuses to stop working. He accepts the fact that the paintings he creates are not the same as before. Like the watercolorist William Thon, who suffered from the same condition, Goldsmith relies on instincts developed over sixty years of working in the medium. "If one is experienced," the painter has written, "he can get to paint, concentrating more on recollection than observation, as I have done."

Reuben Tam once wrote, "I intend my paintings to be statement, reference, evocation, and celebration." Goldsmith would agree with this mission. He also seeks the essence of nature, its simplification and freshness, harmony, rhythm, lyricism, and intensity. His watercolors are acts of brilliant fusion: of nature, passion, and perception.

NOTES

In writing this appreciation, the author drew on a series of interviews he conducted with Lawrence Goldsmith and his wife, Lynda, over two days in June 2003. He also relied on taped interviews made by Doris Birmingham, professor of art history at Framingham State College, and Edward Deci, director of the Monhegan Museum. The Birmingham interview took place in Bow, New Hampshire, in November 1993. The interview with Deci was recorded in Goldsmith's Monhegan studio on August 19, 2002.

1. Samuel Adams Drake, *The Pine Tree Coast*. (Boston: Estes and Lauriat, 1891) 207.

2. Born in Mexico City and raised in Los Angeles, Mario Cooper (1905–1995) was an illustrator, watercolorist, and sculptor. Like Goldsmith, he studied at the Grand Central School of Art. He illustrated for *Collier's* and was the author of several books on watercolor technique, including *Flower Painting in Water Color* (1962).

3. Louise Dickinson Rich, *The Coast of Maine: An Informal History and Guide*. (Camden, Maine: Down East Books, 1993 reprint) 246.

4. Bellows to Emma Bellows, 9 August 1911, Bellows Papers (Box 1, Folder 3), Special Collections Department, Amherst College Library, Amherst, Massachusetts.

5. Nordness, Lee, editor, and Allen S. Weller, text, *Art USA Today*. New York: The Viking Press, 1963, vol. II, 309.

6. Goldsmith refers to this group as the "New York School on Monhegan" because many of the artists lived in and around the city during the winter. He was younger than many of them. "I miss them," he said in an interview; "No one is really taking their place."

7. Eliot O'Hara, *Making Watercolor Behave*. (New York: Minton, Balch and Company, 1932) 22.

8. The "Jamie" in the title is the painter Jamie Wyeth, Goldsmith's next-door neighbor on Monhegan.

9. O'Hara, *Making Watercolor Behave*, 34.

10. "Suddenly blue sky opened above, and to the northwest sunlight struck down to the sea, brightening the wave crests and darkening their blue. Abeam, a billow of fog wavered, split, and rose. The sun vanished behind it and the water darkened, but there appeared, two or three miles away, a red cliff with its rugged base in white foam. The curtain of gray lifted higher. . . . Islandia! I had seen the naked rock of her shores . . . . " Austin Tappan Wright, *Islandia*. (Woodstock, New York: The Overlook Press, 2001) 27.

11. The artist likes to tell the story of the couple visiting Monhegan. While the husband has achieved his ambition of visiting the island, the wife complains loudly, "Too many artists, too many rocks."

12. "All of the northern coastal plain was drowned. Some of its more elevated parts are now offshore shoals, the fishing banks off the New England and Canadian coasts—Georges, Browns, Quereau, the Grand Bank. None of it remains above the sea except here and there a high and isolated hill, like the present island of Monhegan, which in ancient times must have stood above the coastal plain as a bold monadnock." Rachel Carson, *The Edge of the Sea*. (Boston: Houghton Mifflin Company, Signet Paperback reprint, no date) 43.

13. M. Stephen Doherty, "Recent Images, Recent Concerns," *Watercolor 92, American Artist* magazine. (New York, 1992) 41.

14. Lawrence Goldsmith, *Watercolor Bold & Free*. (New York, NY: Watson Guptill, first paperback edition, 2000) 10.

PLATES

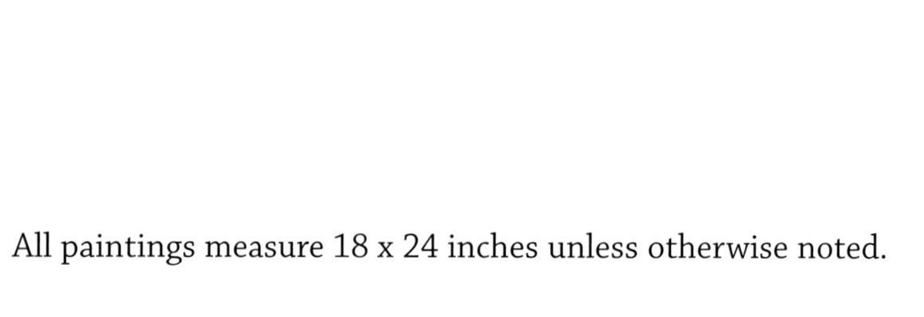

All paintings measure 18 x 24 inches unless otherwise noted.

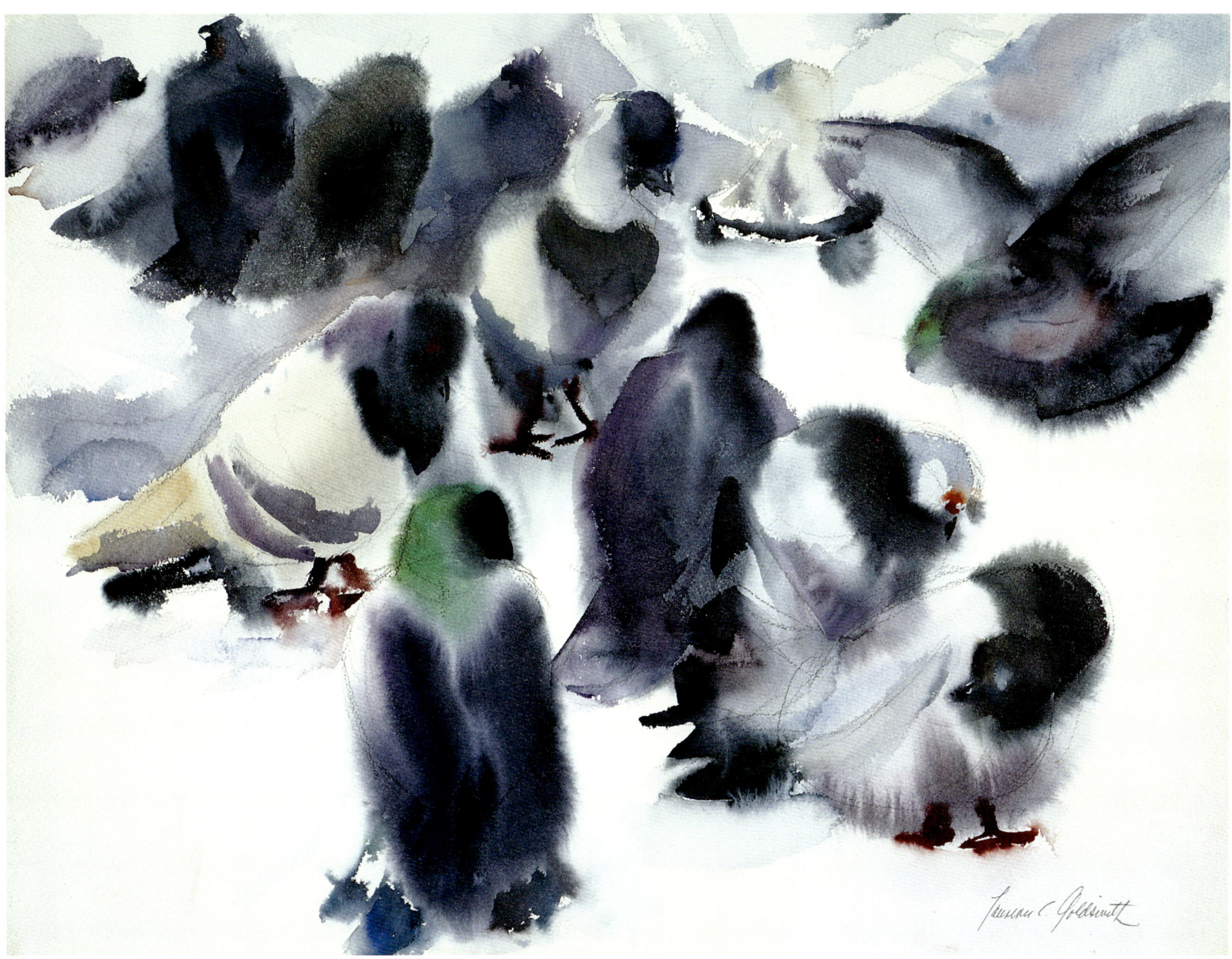

1 *City Dwellers,* ca 1960. Greenwich Village, New York.
Pigeons are as symbolic as anything of the city. They provided one of my last urban subjects.

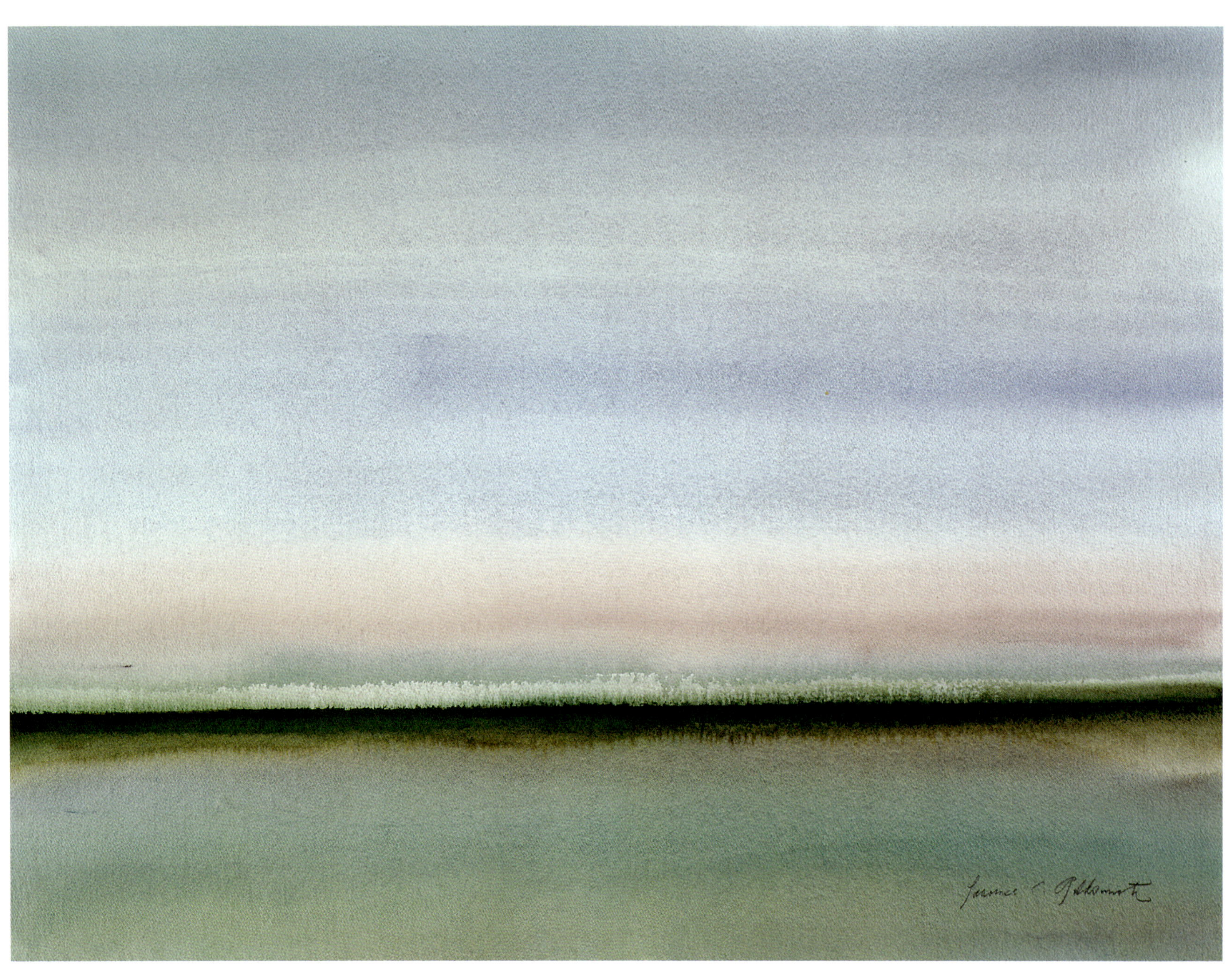

2 *Travelogue 8*, 1996. Watercolor with colored pencil. Subject matter has faded from view, though the horizontal lines suggest land, sea, sky, horizon.

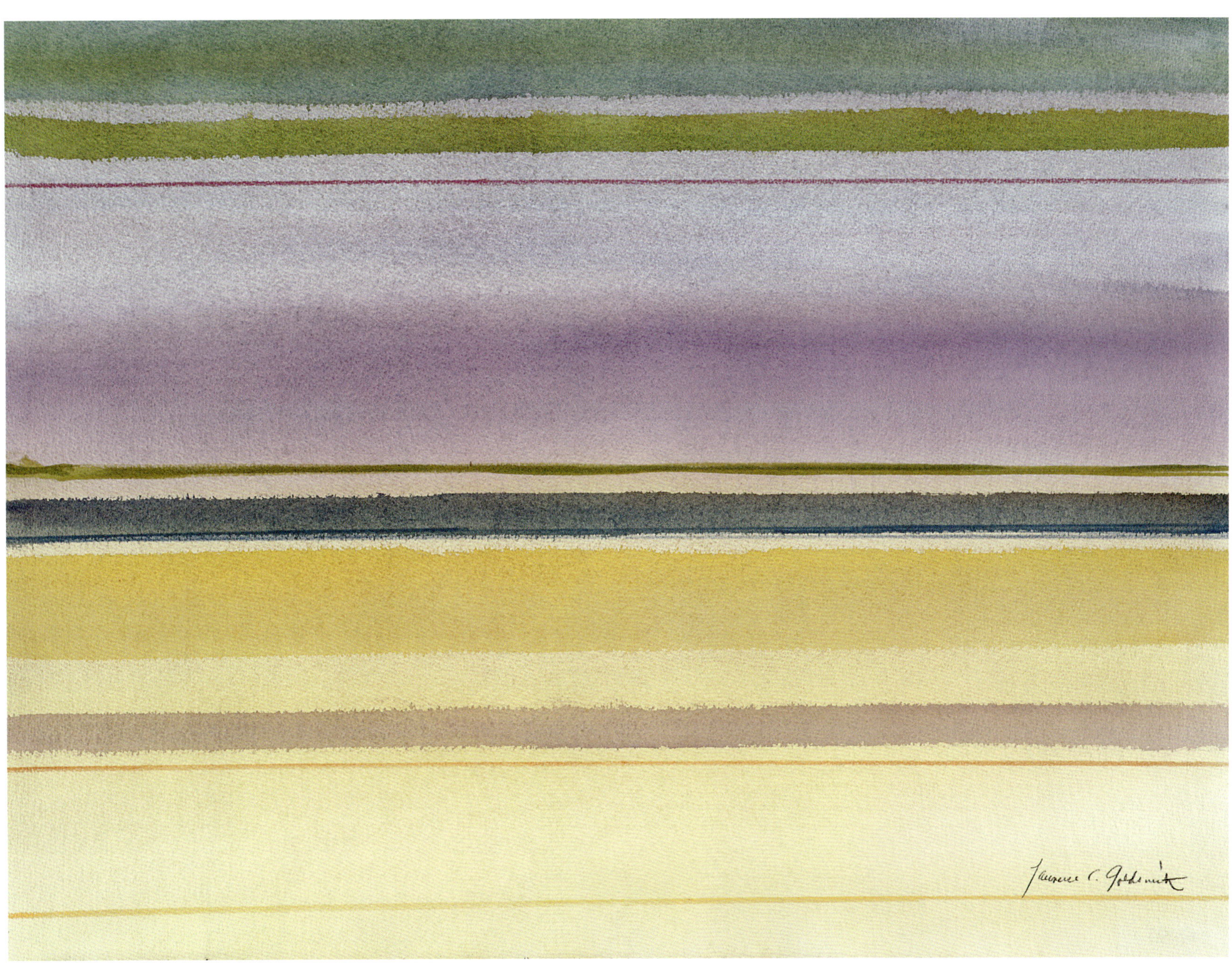

3 *Travelogue 32,* 1997. Horizontal bars can be placed in an infinite assortment of arrangements. Mark Rothko became famous for his inventions, which he controlled with vertical borders. I worked in a more modest field.

4 *Voyageur 8,* 1997. Watercolor with colored pencil.

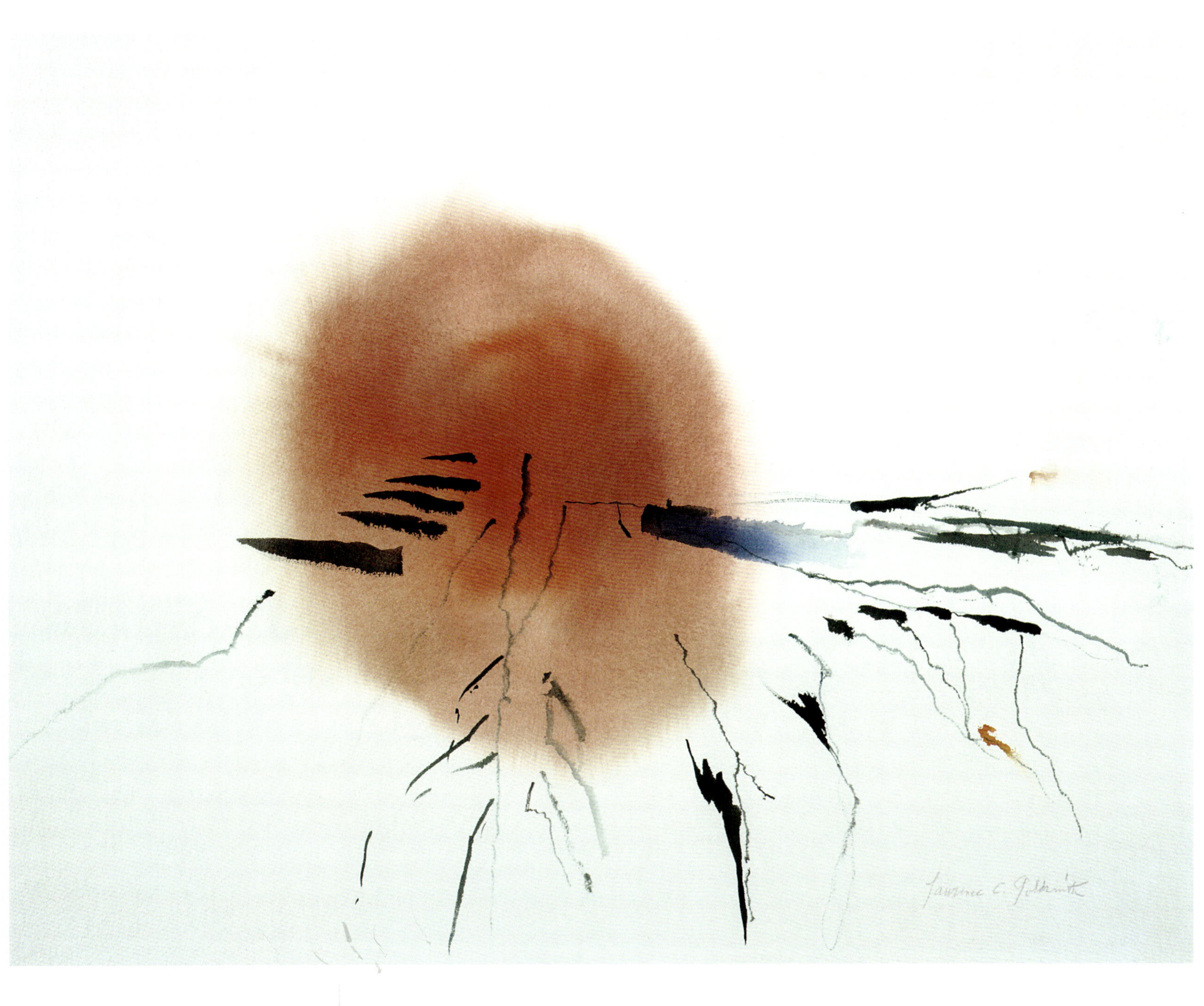

5 *Hot Spot,* 2000. Collection of Elizabeth Skarie.

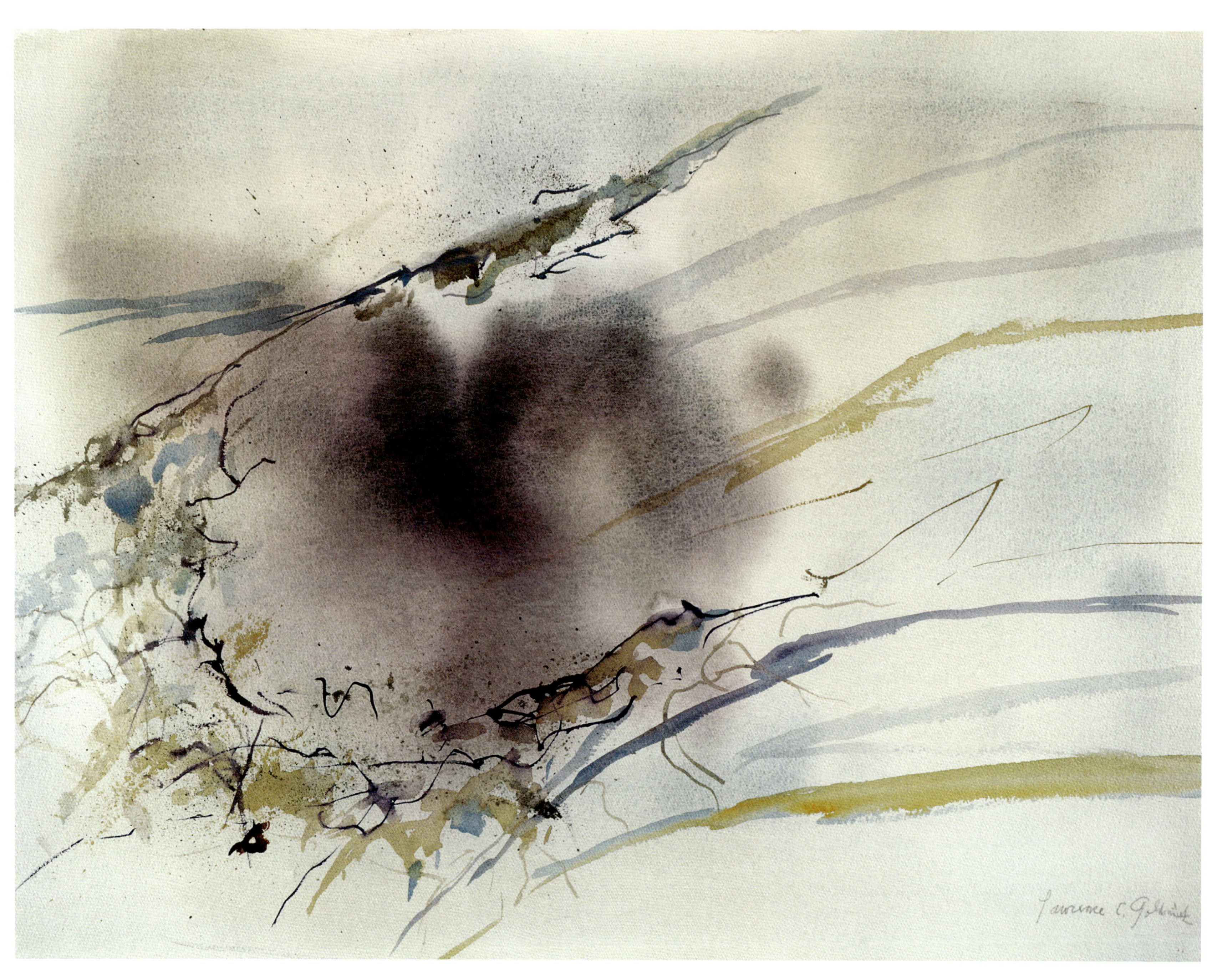

6 *From Jamie's Bench,* 2002. A favorite resting place on Monhegan, the bench is a perch from which to confront the moods of the ocean close-up

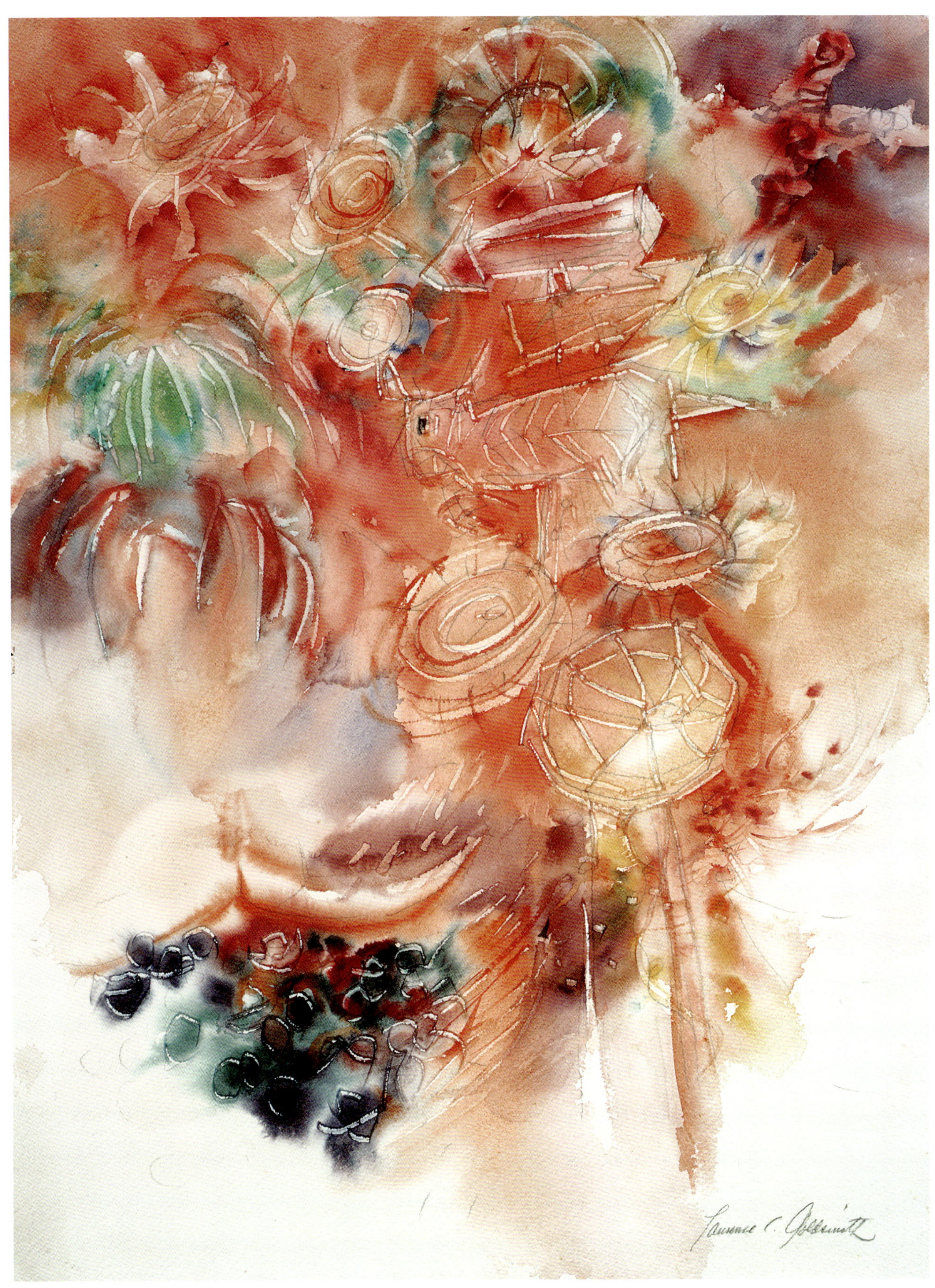

7 *Castillo* (Night of Fireworks), 1972. 24 x 18 in. Ajijic, Jalisco, Mexico. A wonderfully festive pastime in Mexico is an evening of sparkling fireworks. The next morning, I tried to recreate the excitement of the whirling bamboo tower as it exploded in many bursts of sparks.

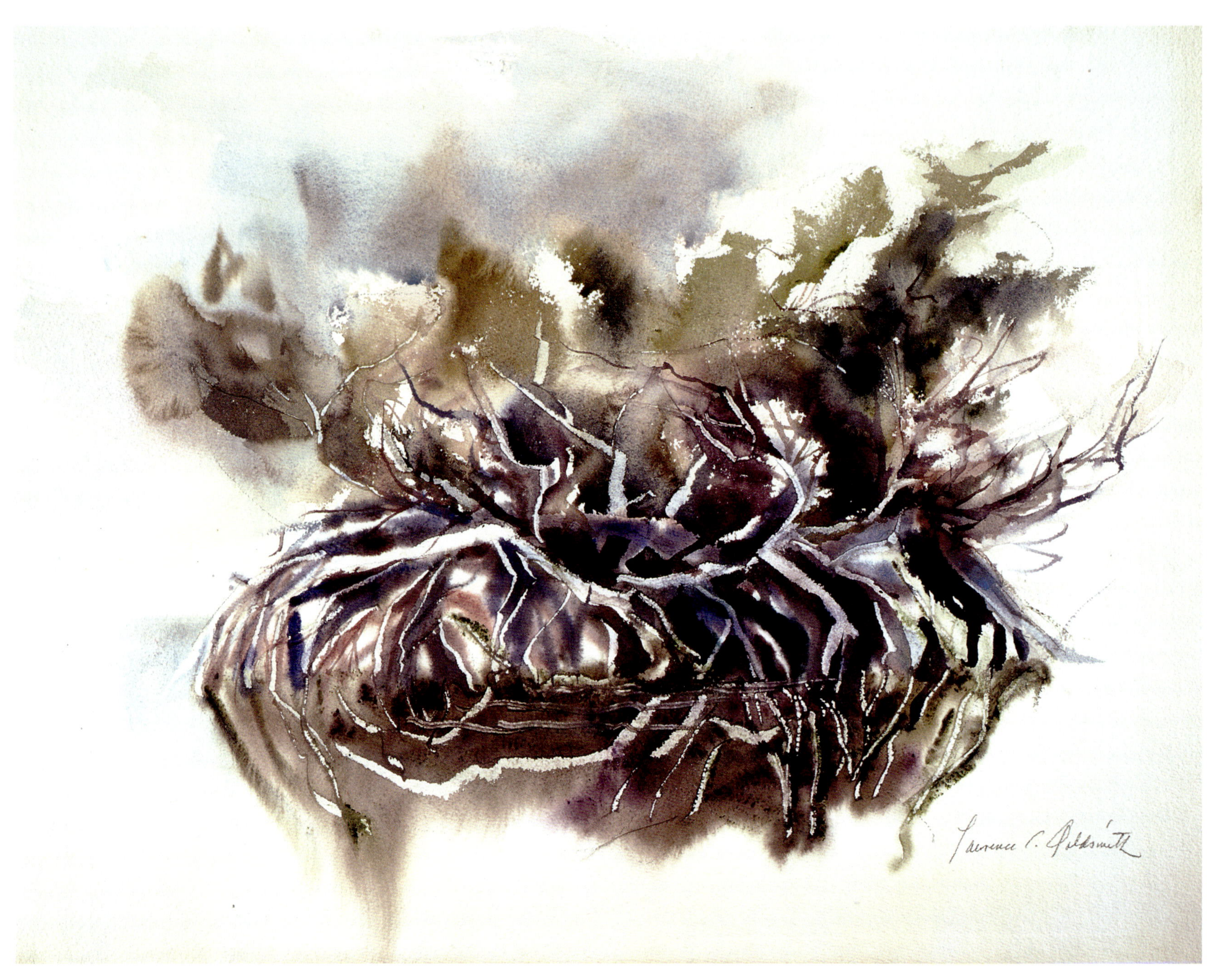

8 *Mangrove Island,* 1972. Sanibel, Florida. The painting shows how the seagoing plants reach out into the sea, converting vegetation into land.

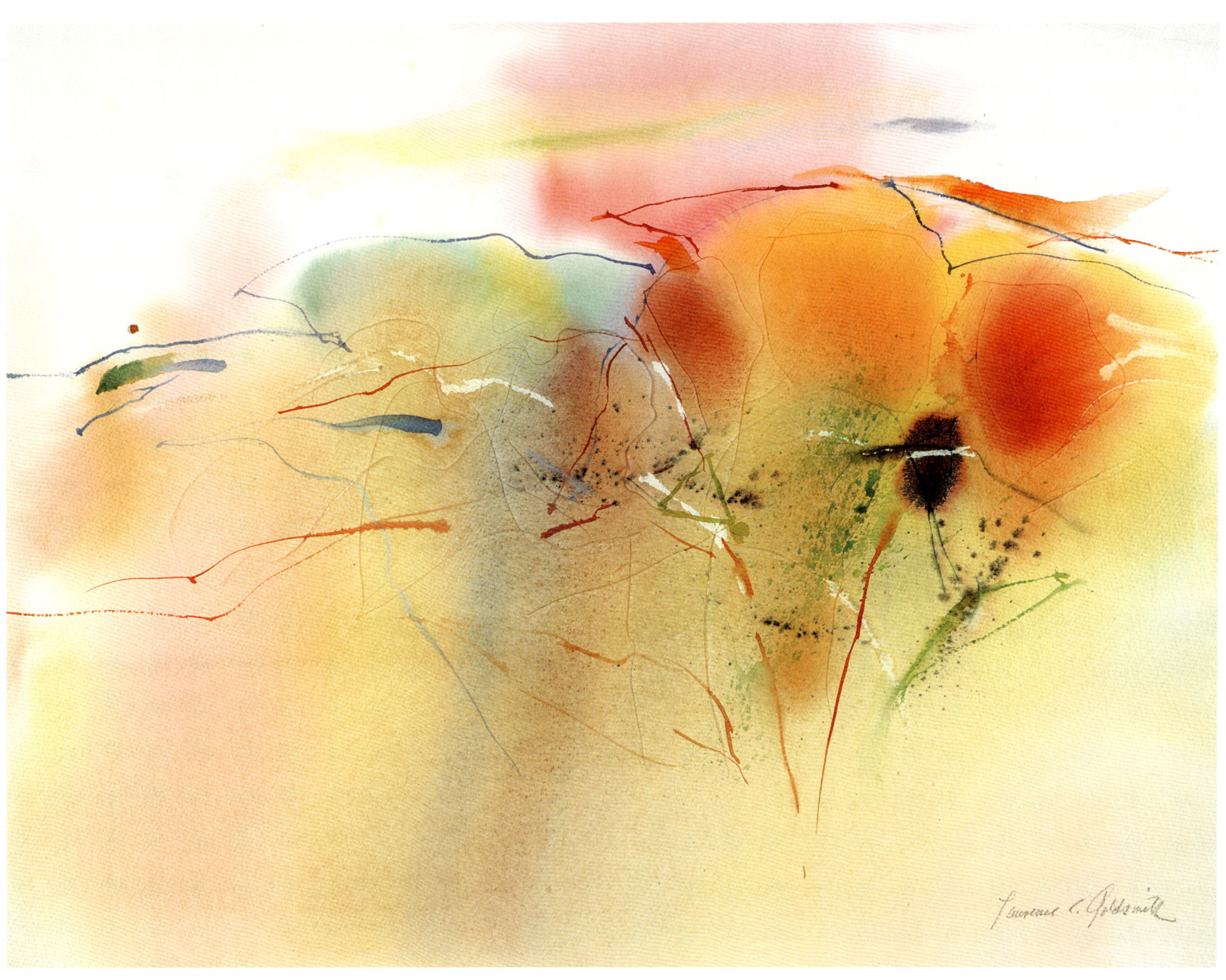

9 *Torrid Memories,* 1989. I painted this in my Vermont studio, surrounded by snow-covered woods as I recalled a trip to the Southwest.

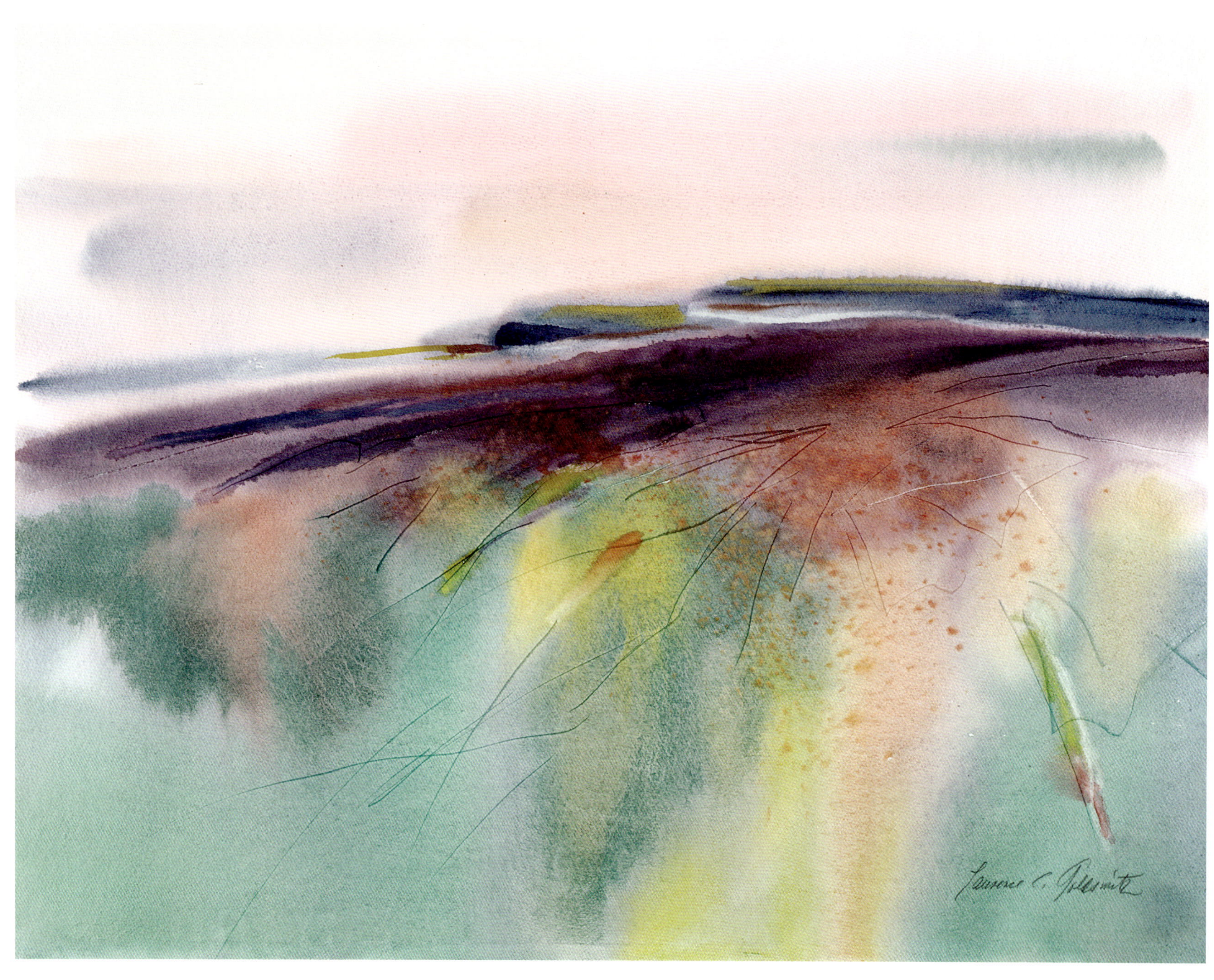

10 *1,000 Miles Away,* 1990. Although I was looking back on a 1,000-mile car trip to Cape Breton Island, the title can be an allusion to almost any faraway place held in the viewer's memory.

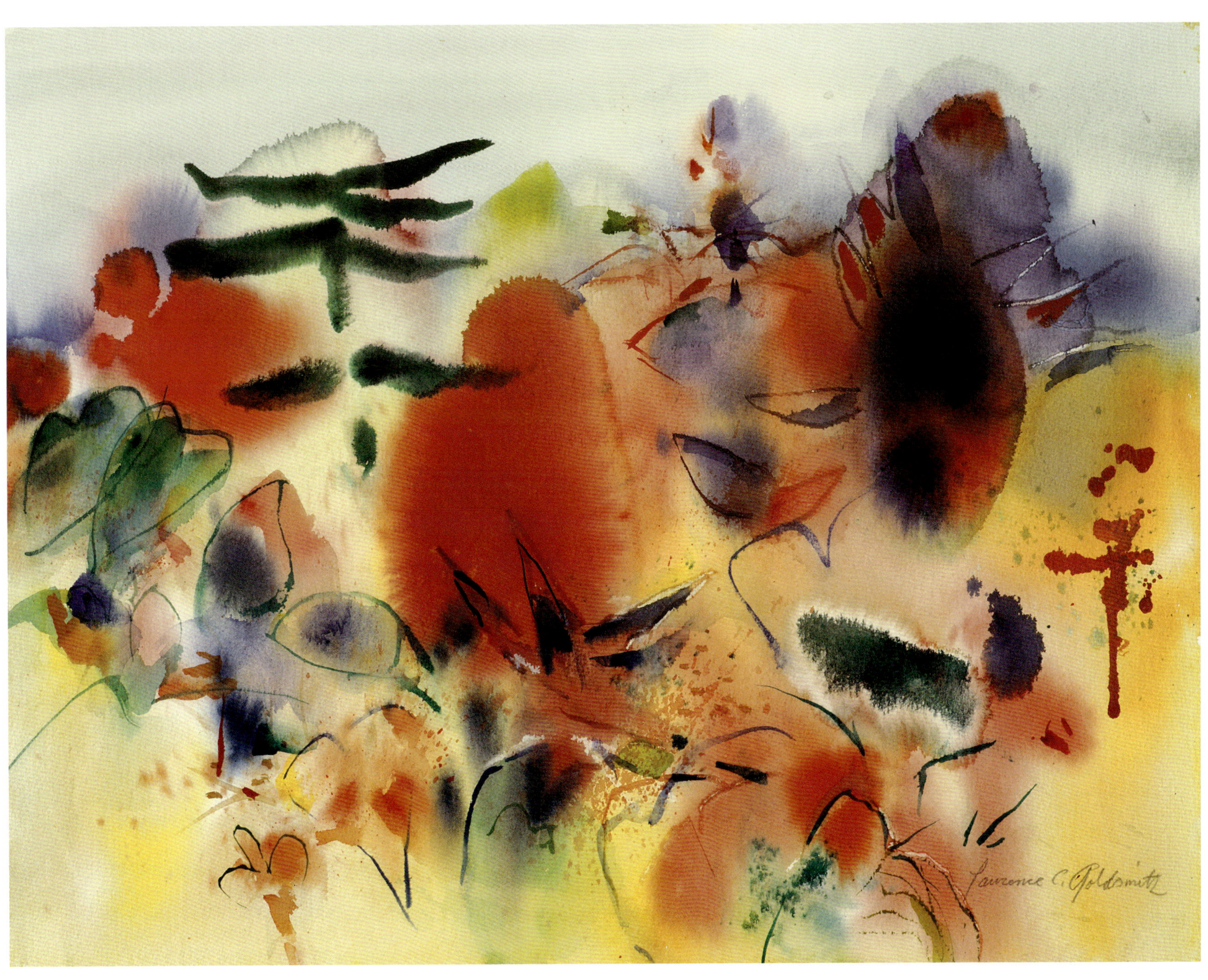

11 *Carib Melody,* 1994. Island of Nevis. This tiny sugar-plantation island, the birthplace of Alexander Hamilton, was once a treasured colonial prize. For me, its jewels lay in the vibrant, undiluted brilliance of the tropical flowers and fruits.

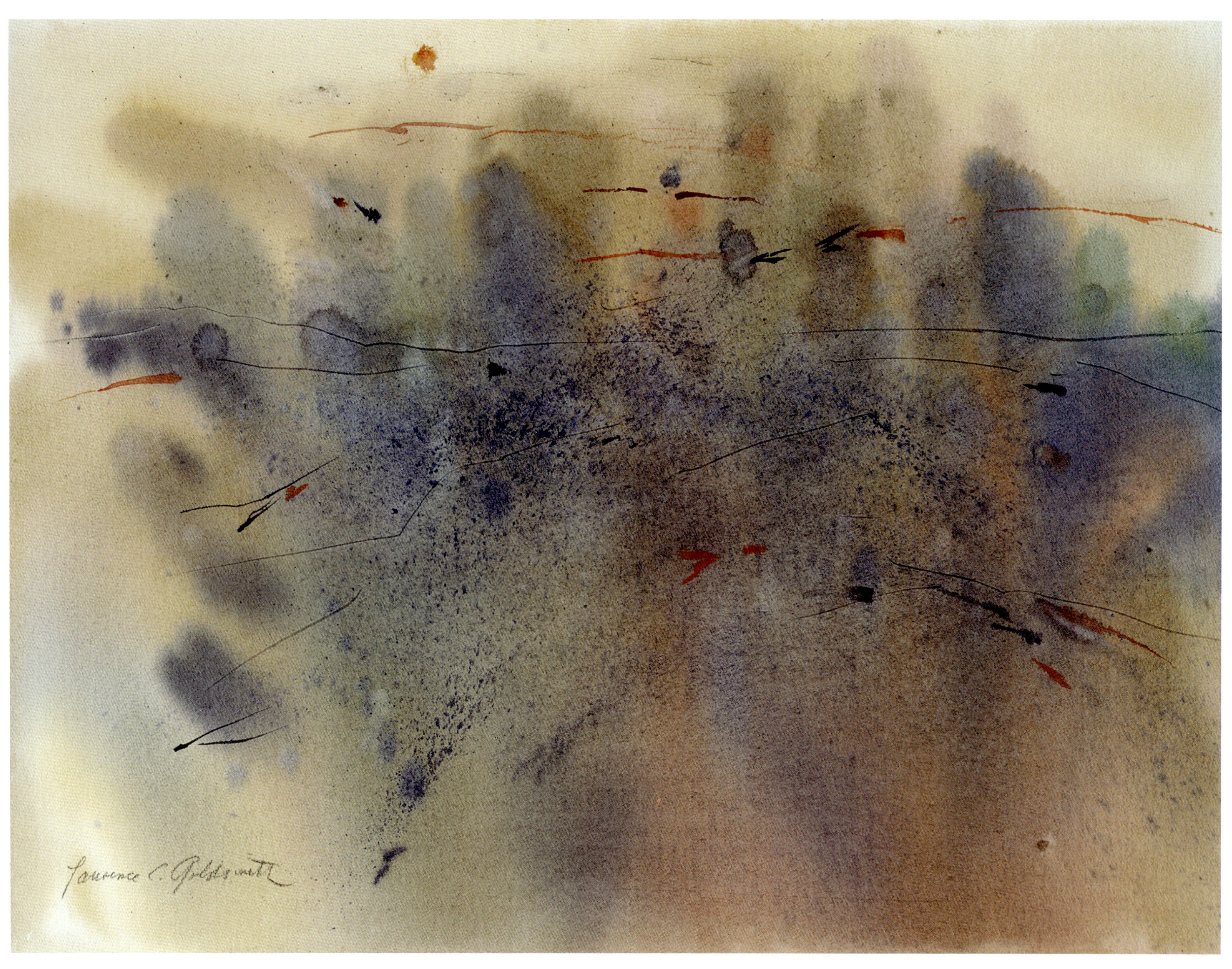

12 *Oriental Legend No. 9*, 1994. One of a series that could be described as unconscious reflections of Southeast Asia. They all fuse together in this airy sweep of Oriental colors and rhythms.

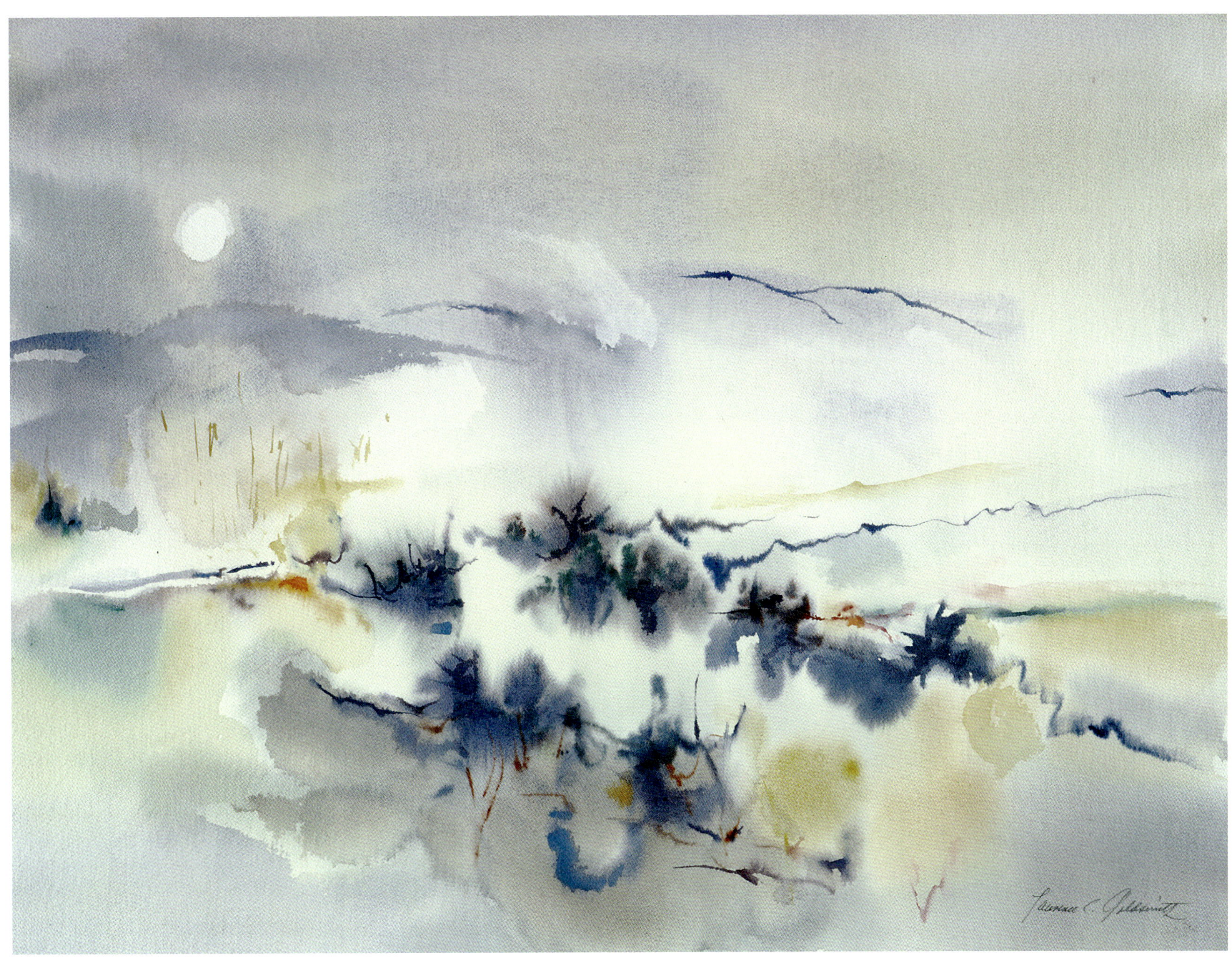

13 *Winter Light in Vermont*, 1973. Vermont winters cast all sorts of colors for the keen eye to discover. The trick is to find subtle color and intensify it.

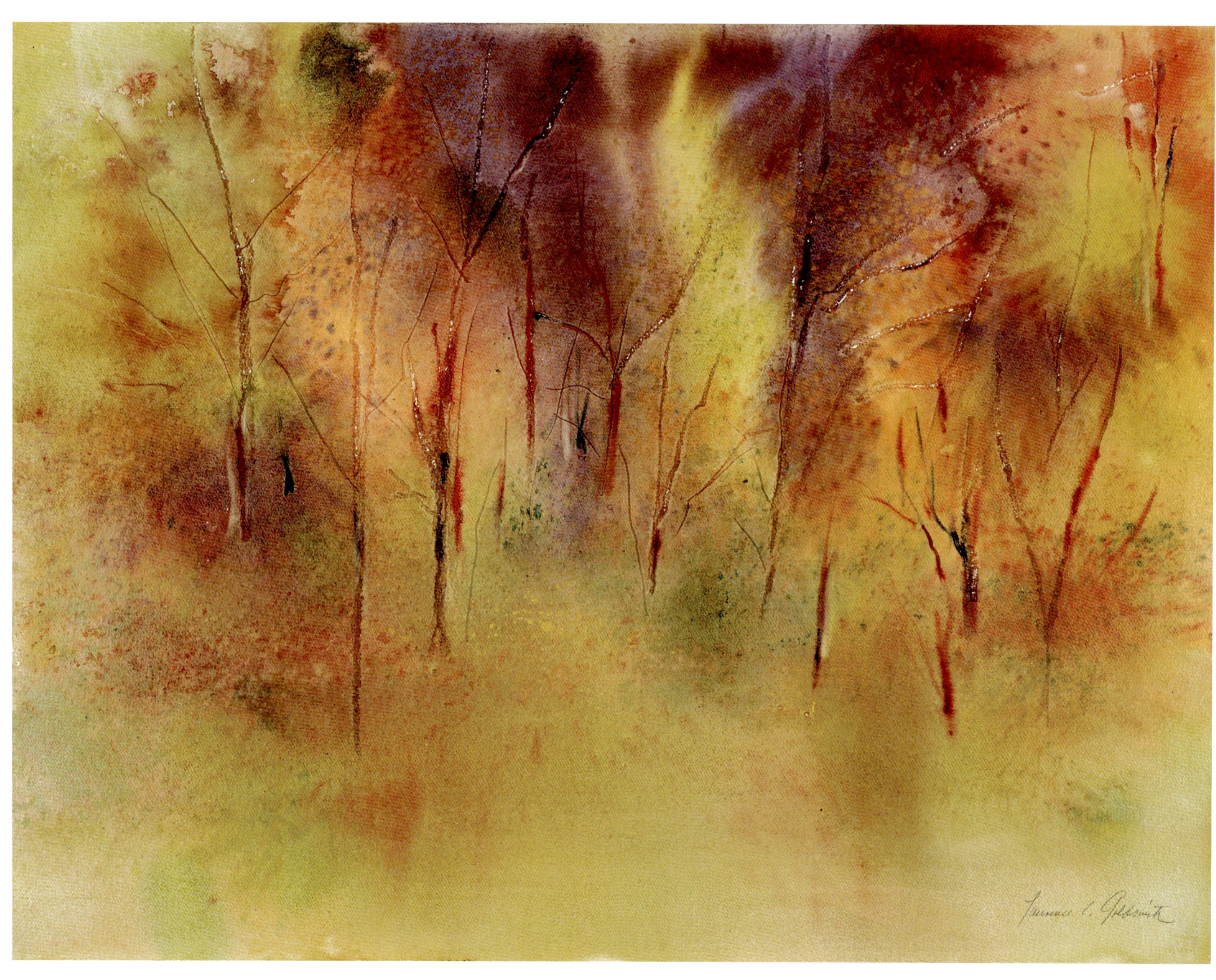

14 *Glittering Woods,* 1975. 22 x 30 in. Venturing the use of a larger sheet than usual, I gave myself room for an abundance of natural shapes and shadows.

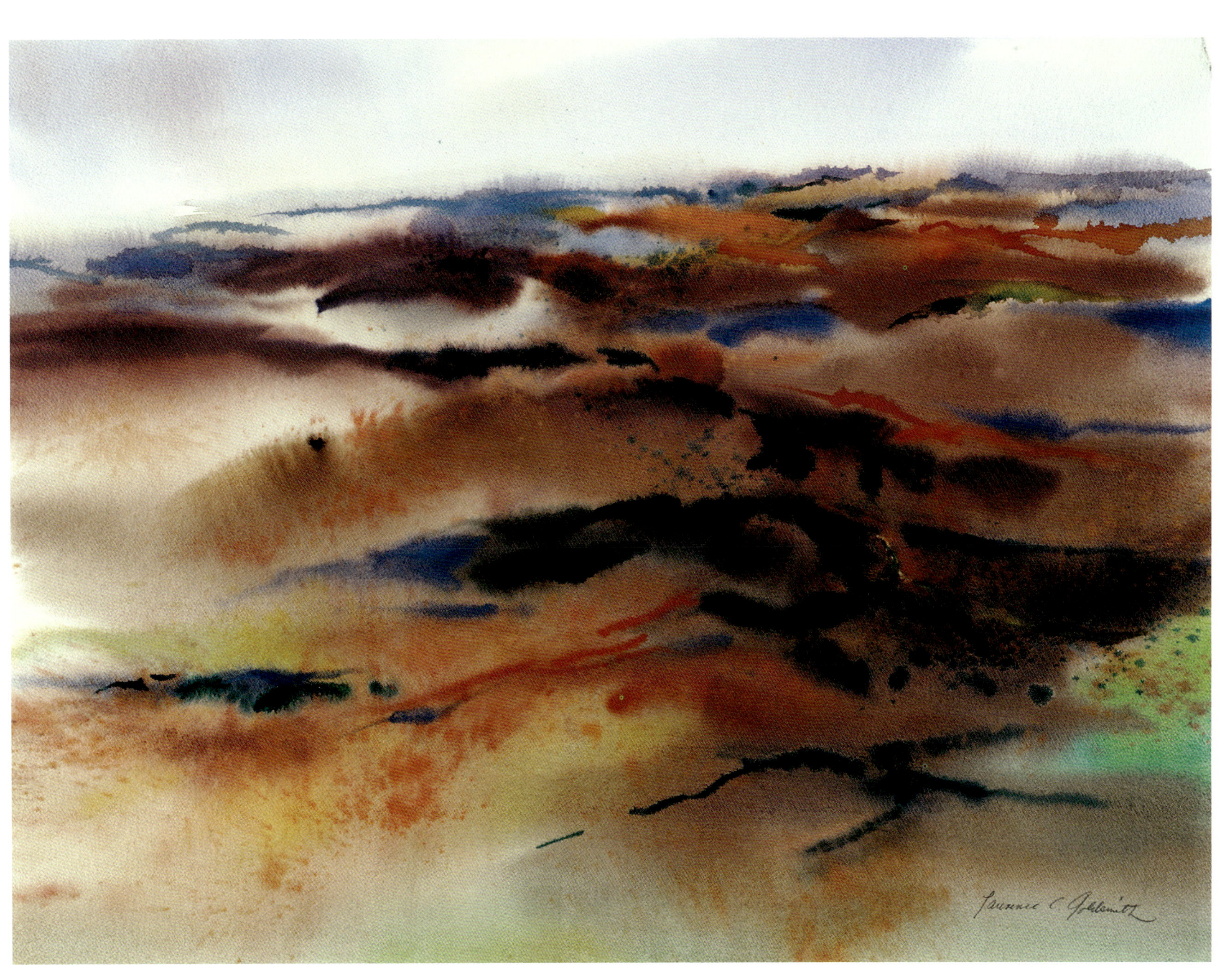

15 *Mountaintop Outlook,* 1978. Mt. Mansfield, Vermont. A wide lateral look from the highest peak in Vermont. The semi-horizontals create great distance, supported by range in color.

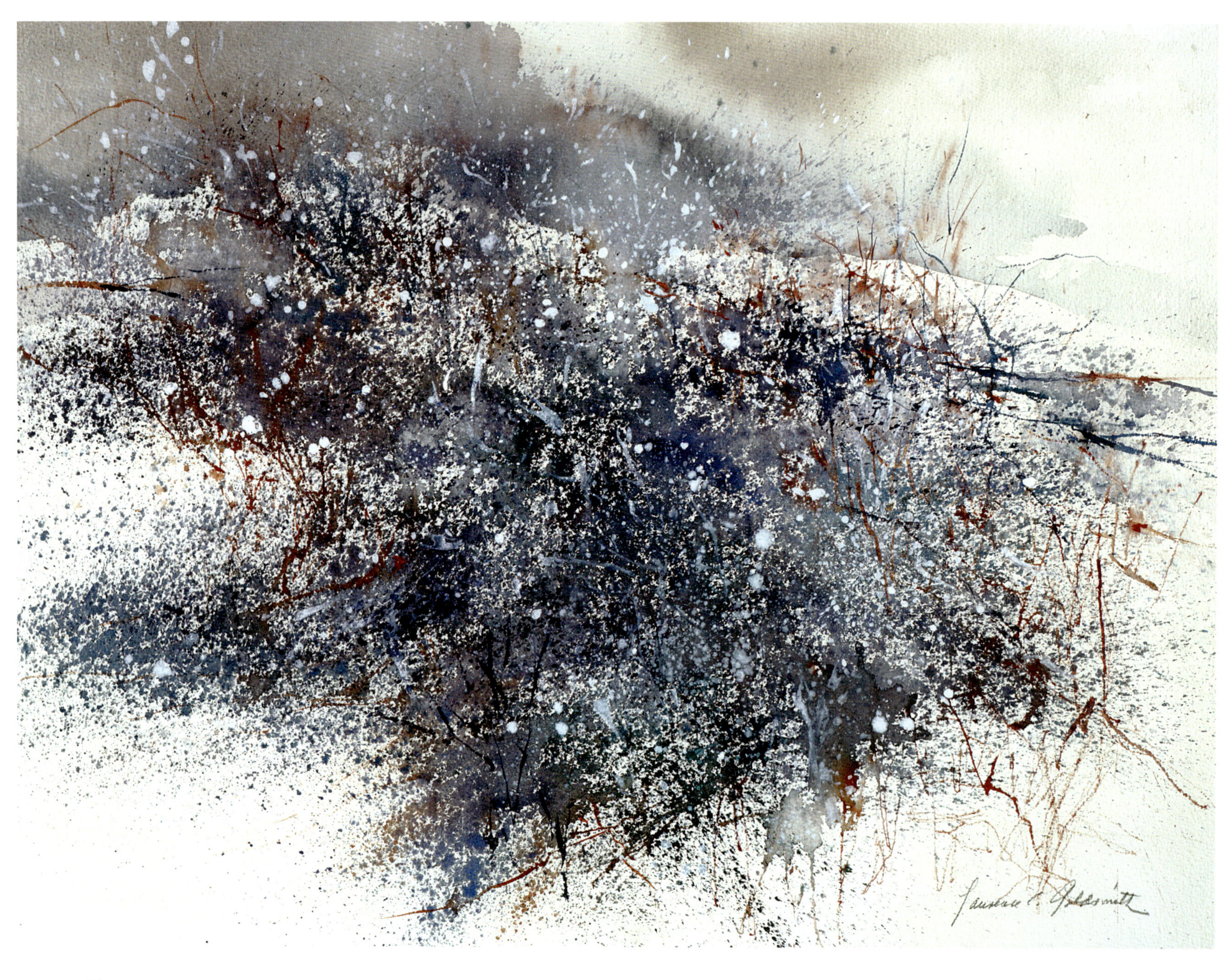

16 *Snowflakes,* 1979. A familiar scene, and yet I sought to rise above the familiar to suggest, perhaps, the balance between the peaceable state of country living and our constant struggle with nature.

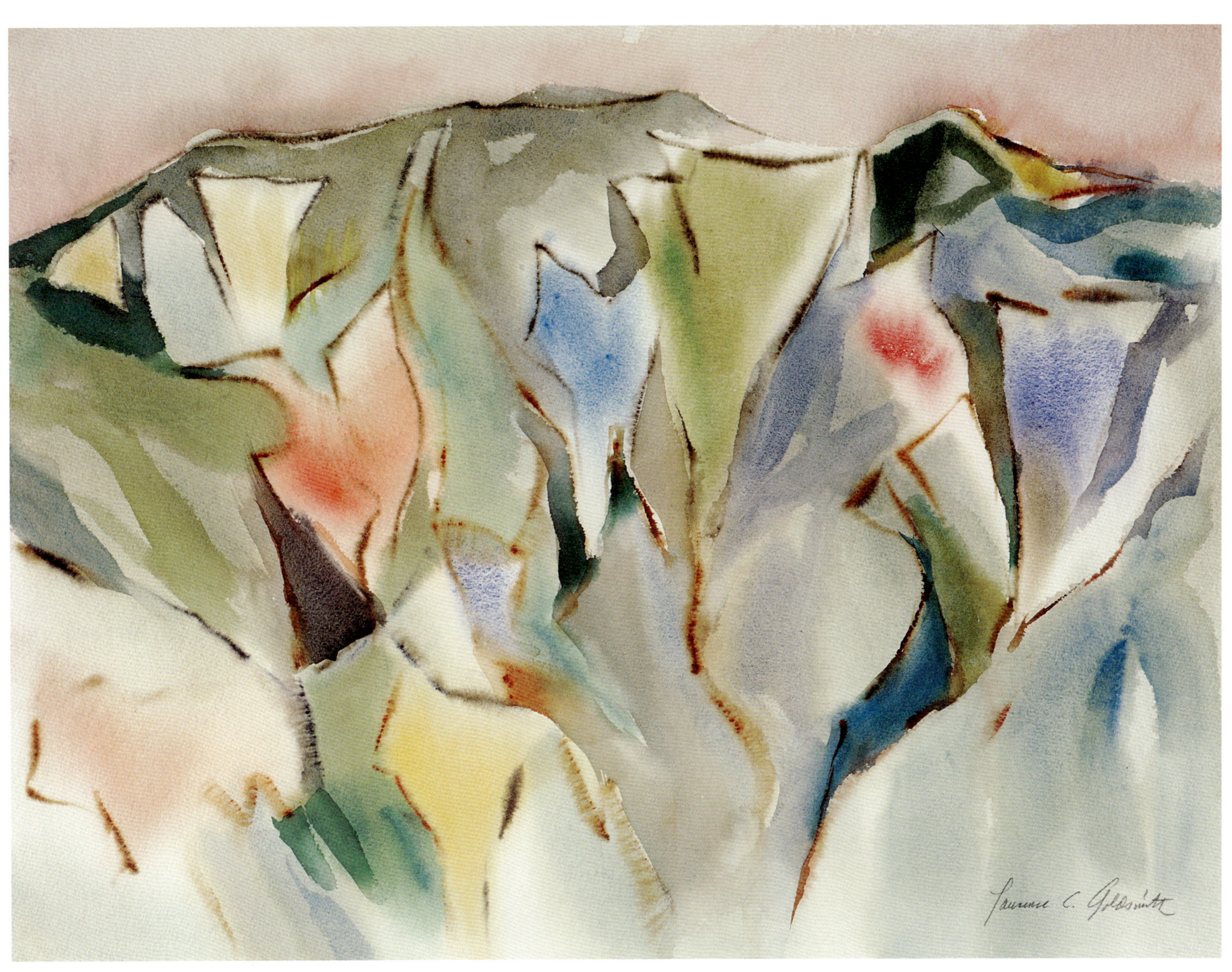

17 *Nature's Jewels,* 1981. Large blocks of color give the impression of a mountain or, in human terms, the might of conviction accreted over the years.

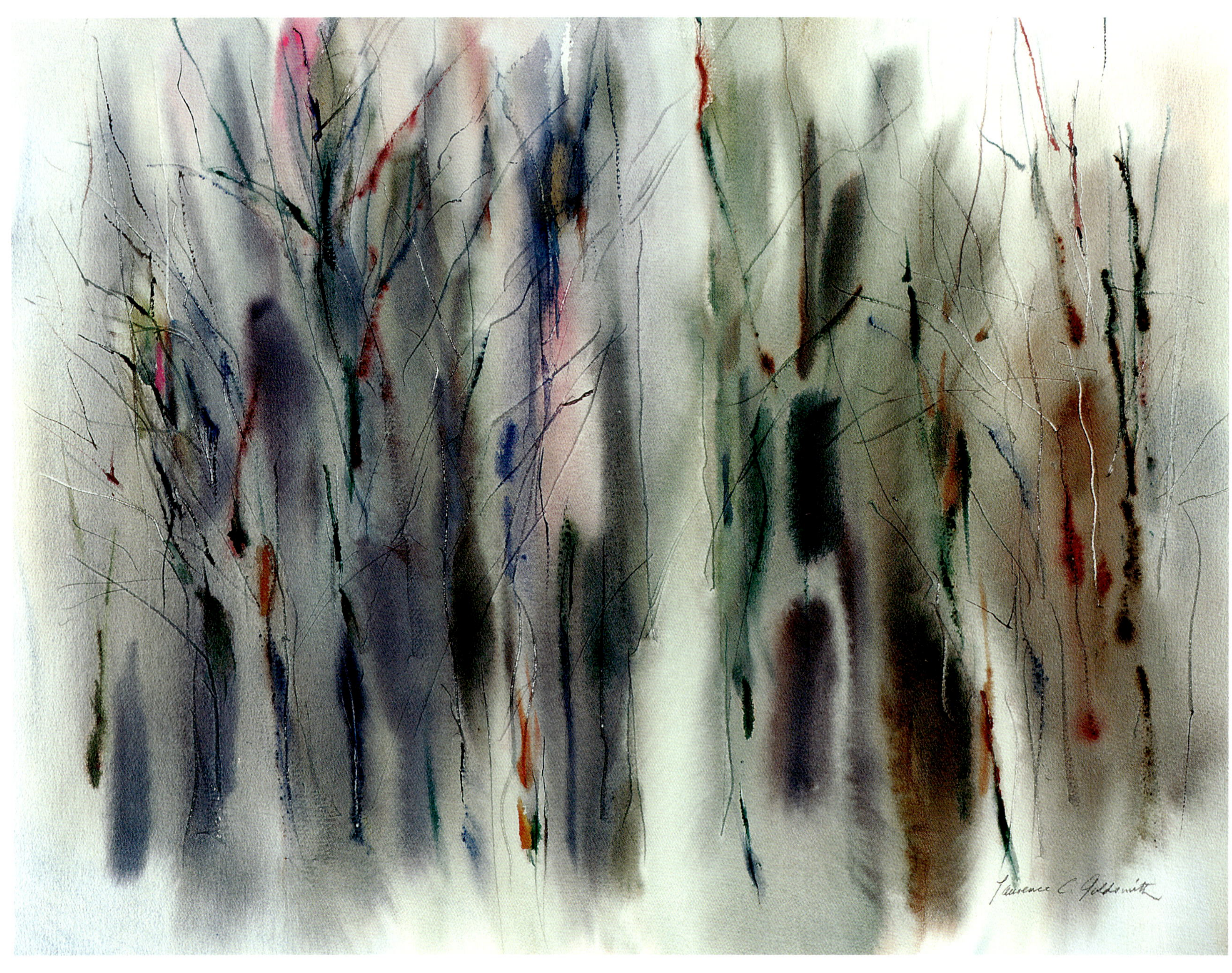

18 *Sounds in the Ravine,* 1985.

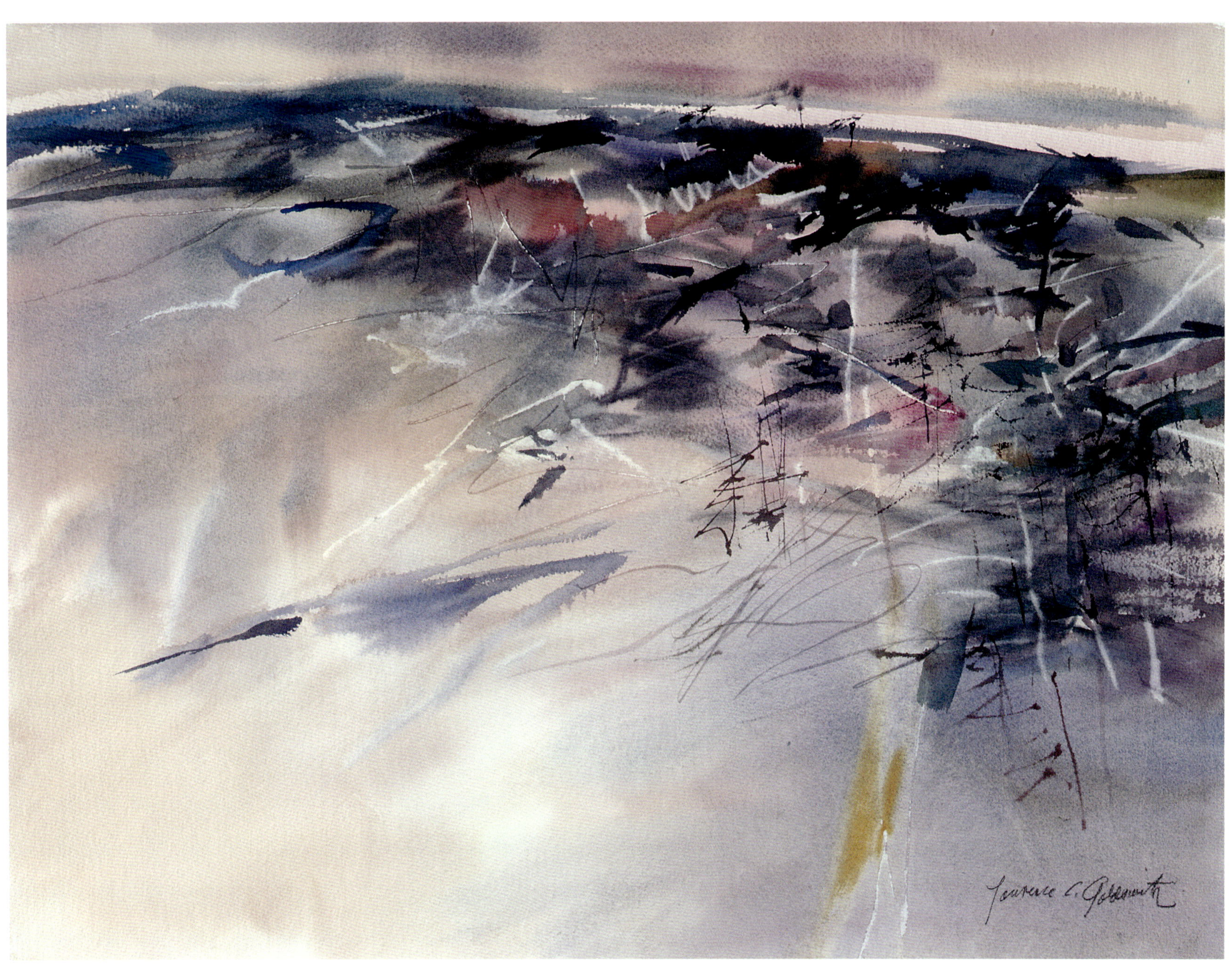

19 *Winter Dawn*, 1996. An example of my use of twists of paper tissue to resemble rough patches of snow. The tissue creates near-white areas when pushed against wet washes.

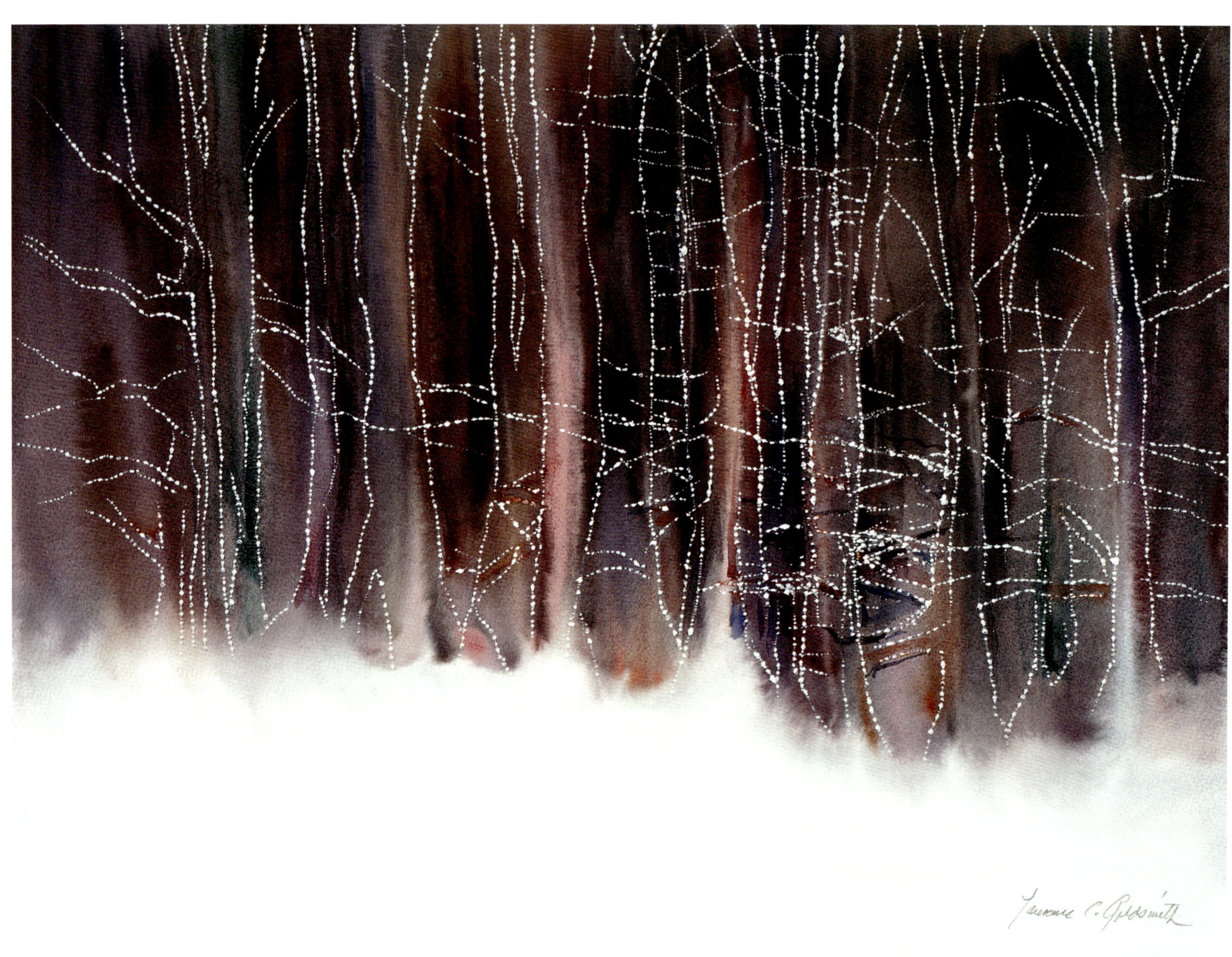

20 *Twig Light,* 1996. Private collection. The bright spots created by scraping with a dental pick add luster to what otherwise would have been a dark woods scene. Those lines bring the composition forward and add motion.

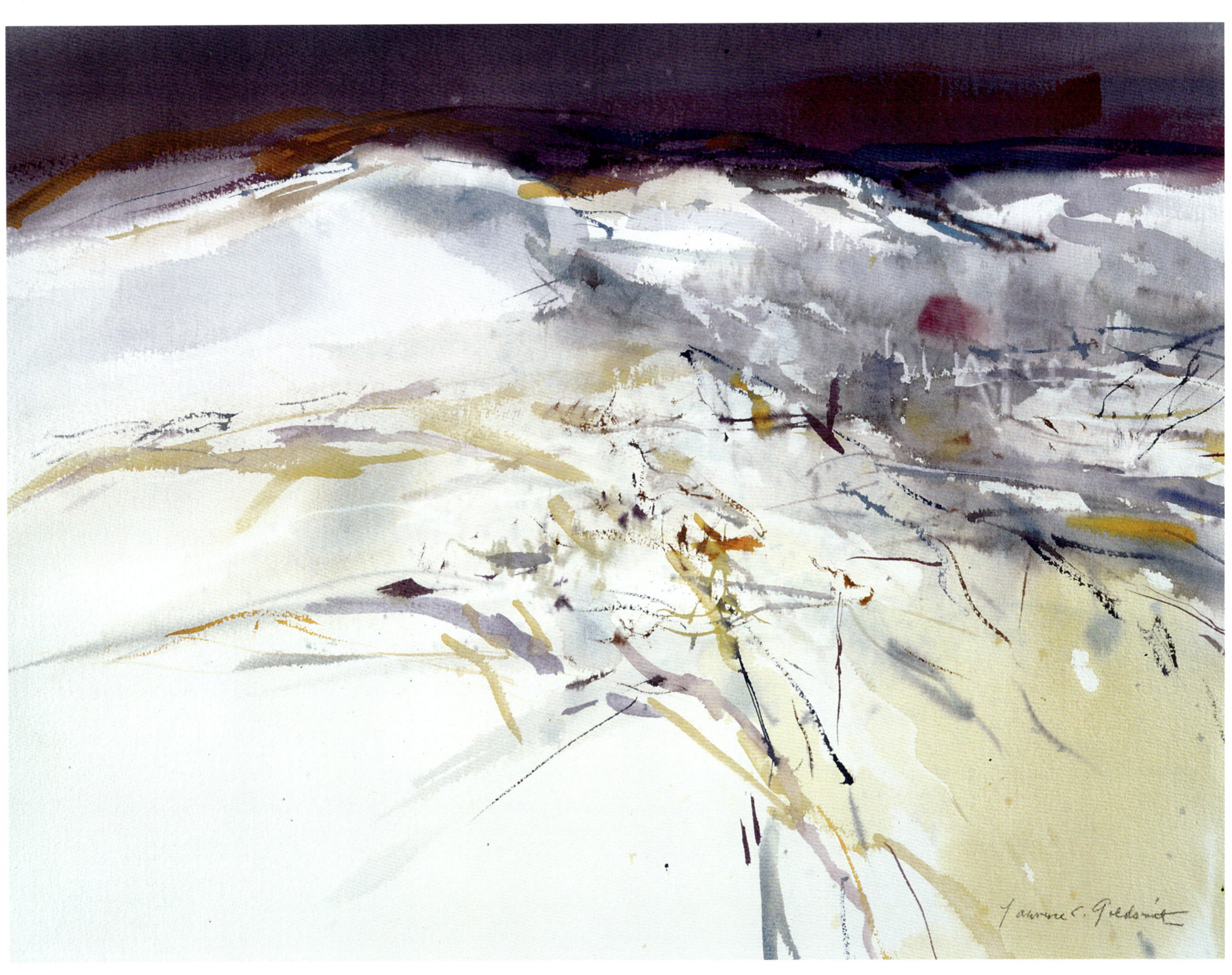

21 *Snow,* 1999. Snow as a subject is very versatile—it is subject to wide interpretation and lends itself well to abstraction.

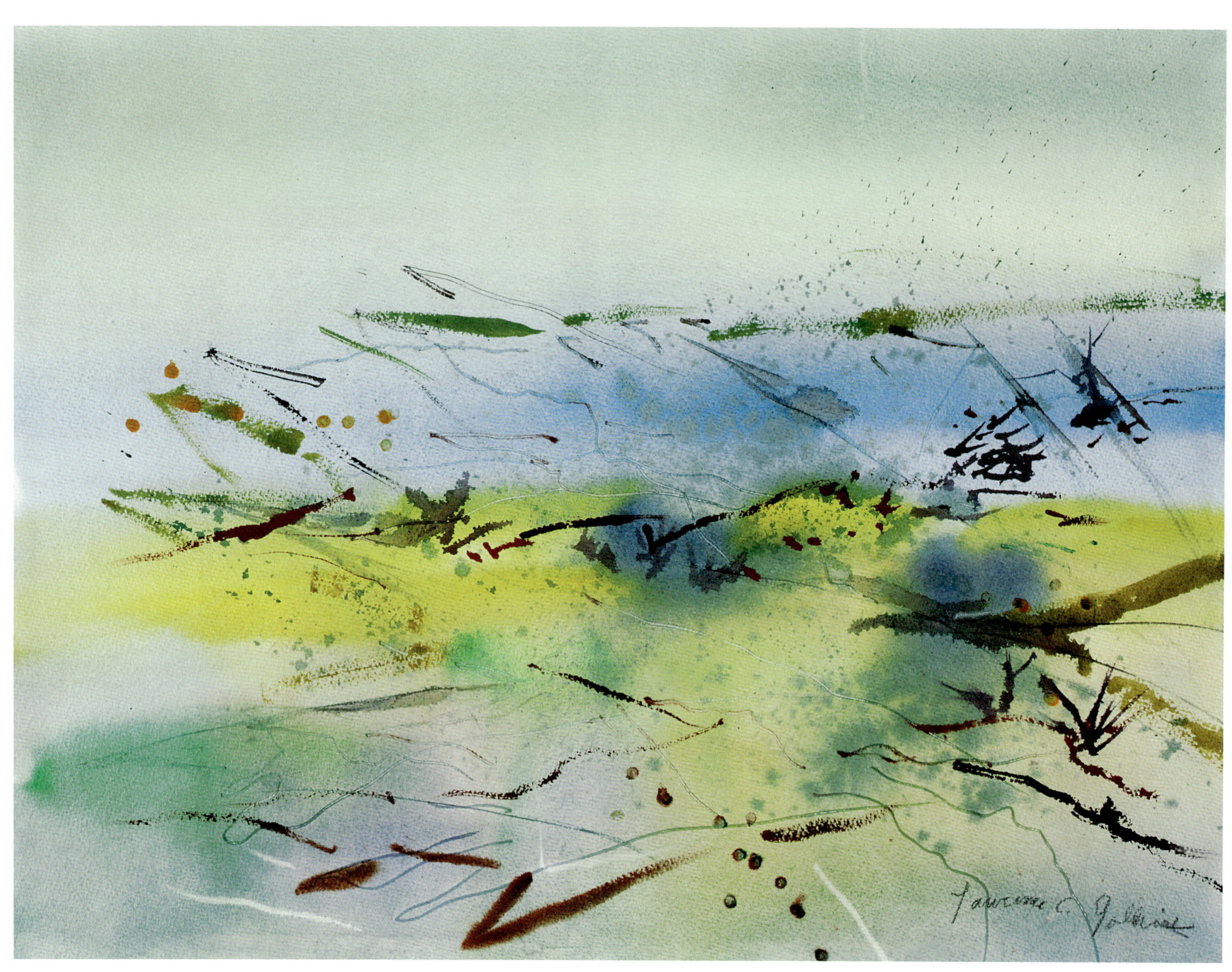

22 *Green Lands,* 2002. Watercolor provides a vast variety of greens, and, as always, I combined a number of pigments in one brushful, making a new green each time. Why not? Vermont is the Green Mountain State.

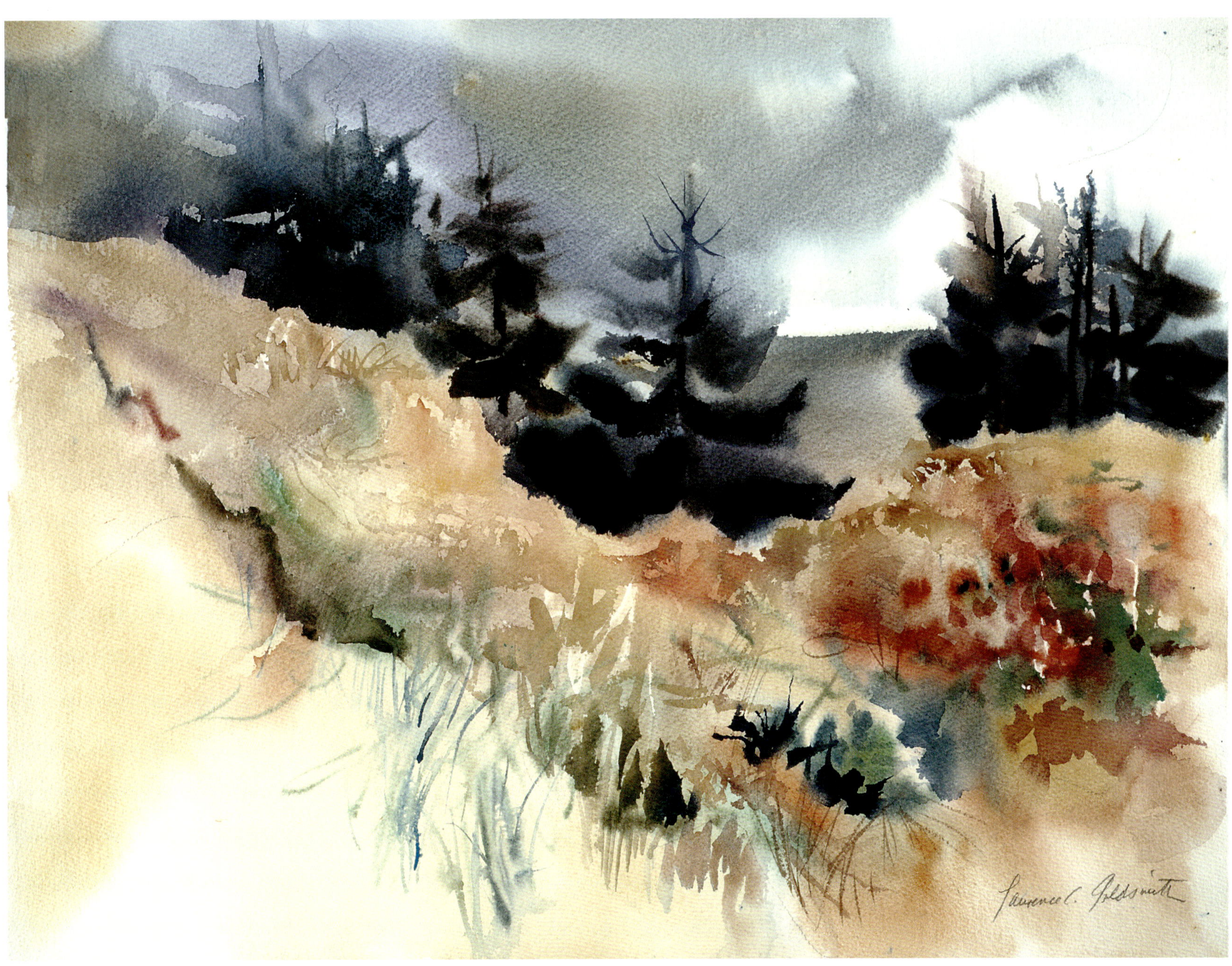

23 *Trail Outlook,* 1963. This painting suggests permanence to me, for the trails and views from them are treasured for their unchanging quality.

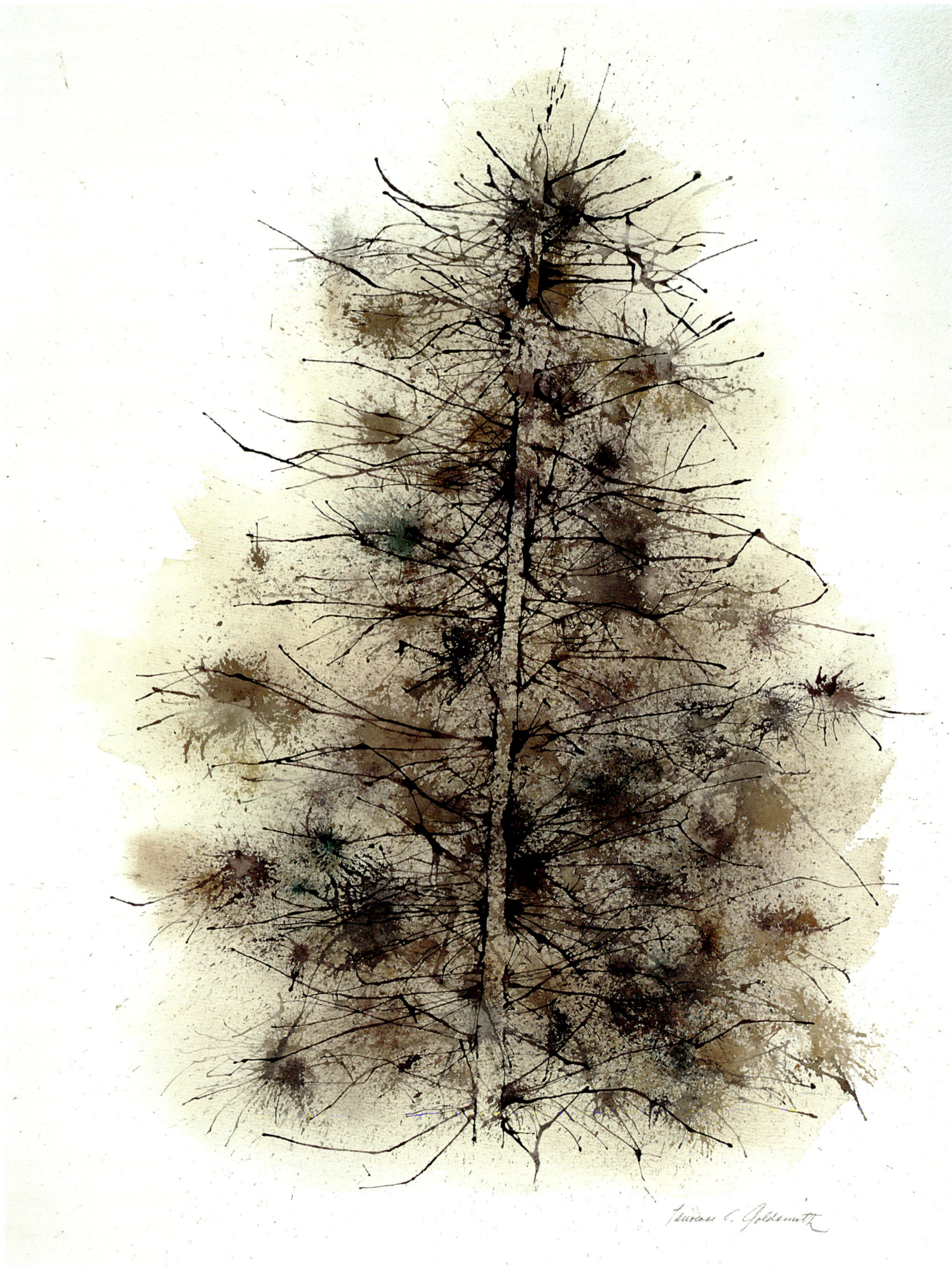

24 *Solo,* 1964. 24 x 19 in. Private collection. Occasionally I confine myself to a monochromatic theme. Here the soaring grandeur of a dead tree gets all the emphasis; dead trees, at least as subject matter, have as much vitality as live ones.

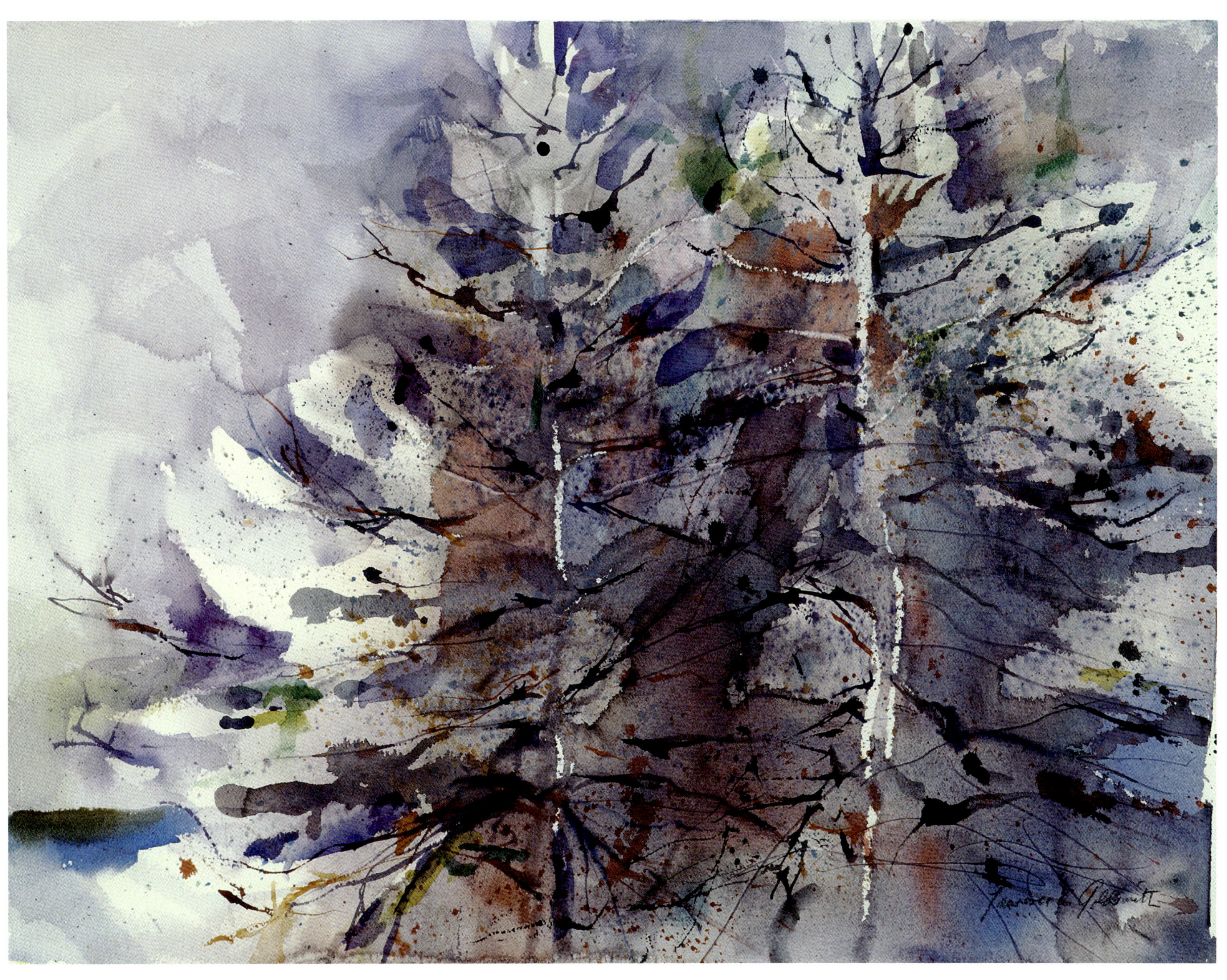

25 *Typical Forest,* 1990.

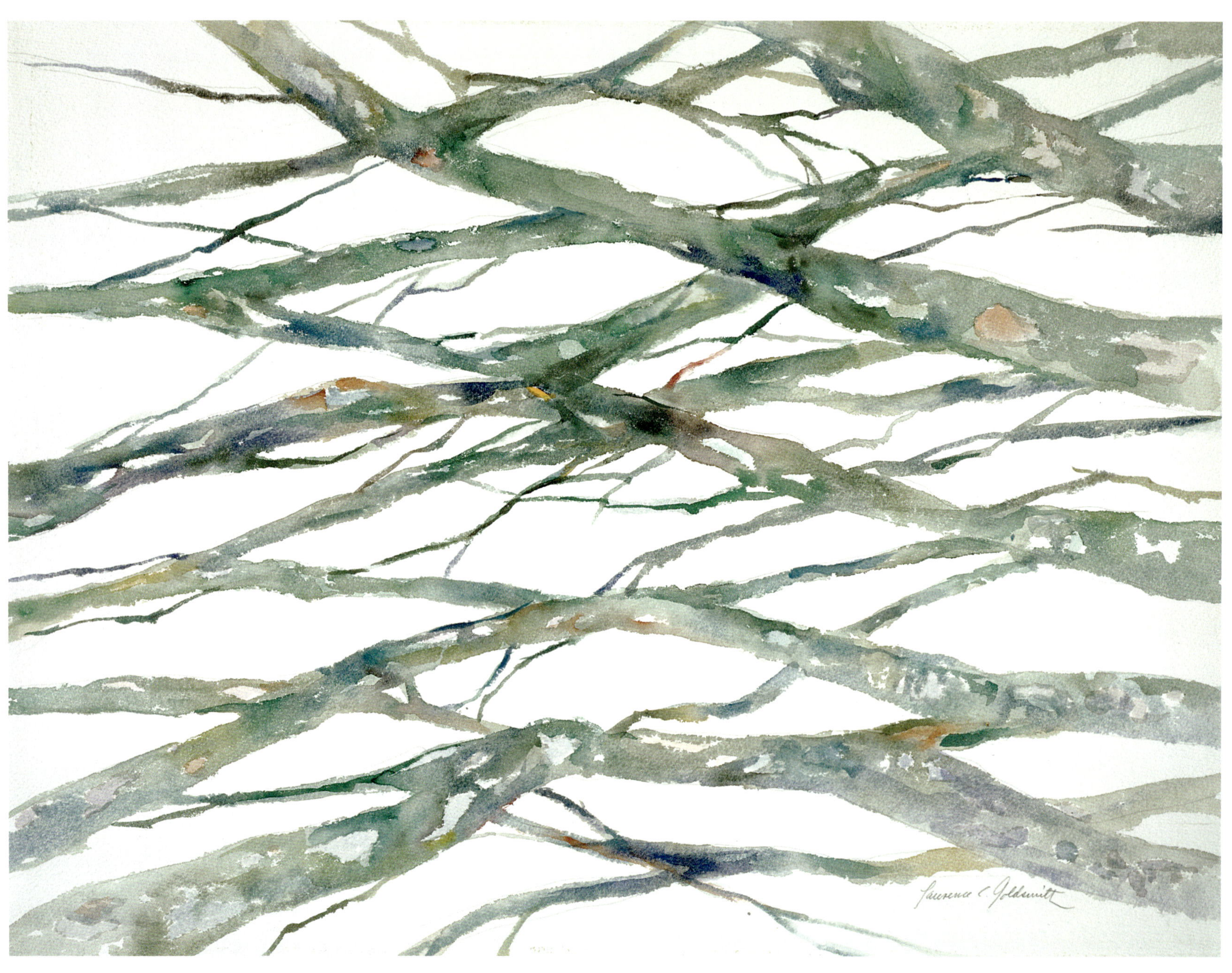

26 *Composed by Studio Window,* 1990. Through a studio window hardly bigger than a watercolor sheet, I captured these lichen-studded branches.

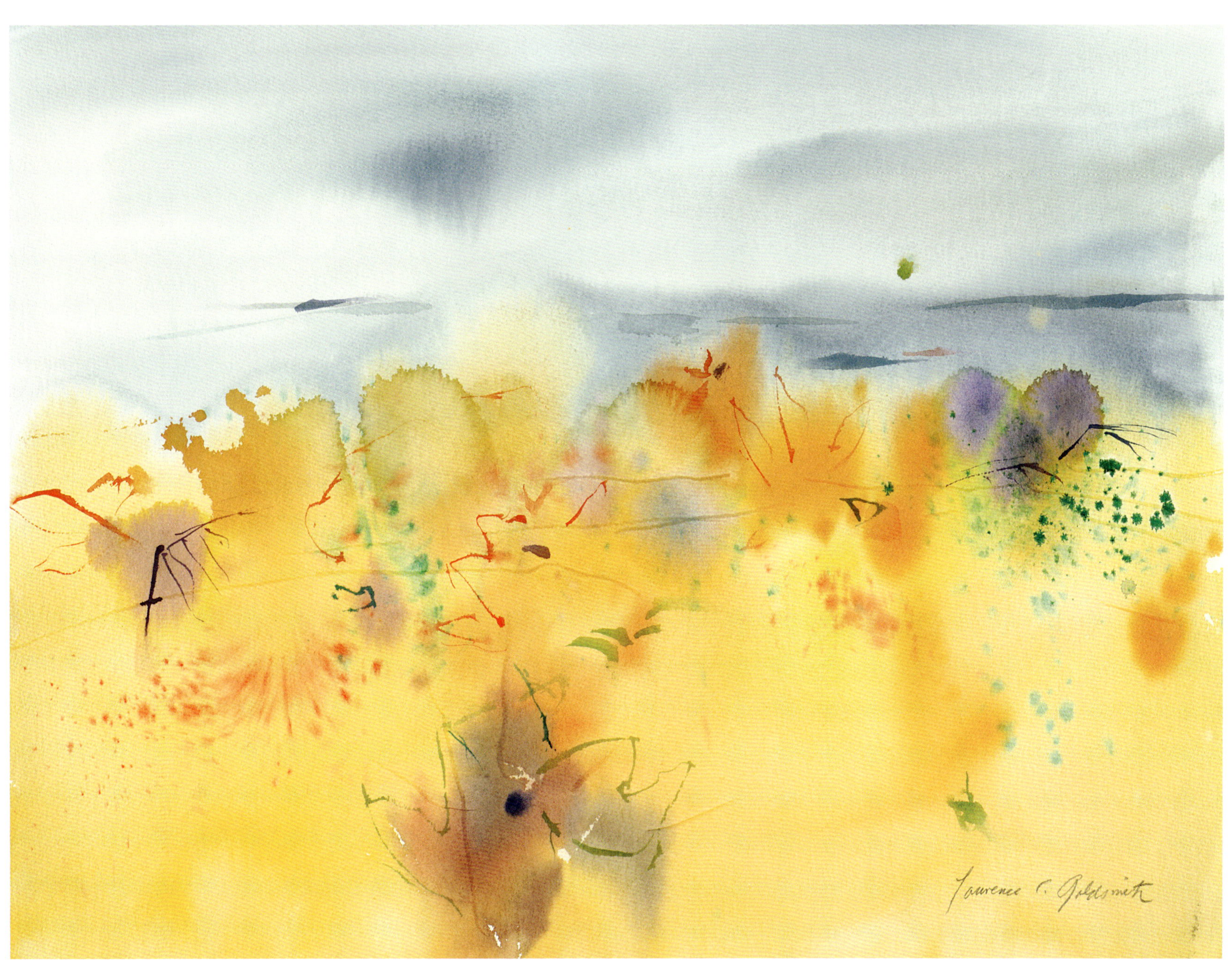

27 *Leeward Yellows,* 1994. I believe that any color can make the base of a successful watercolor painting provided it dominates without question.

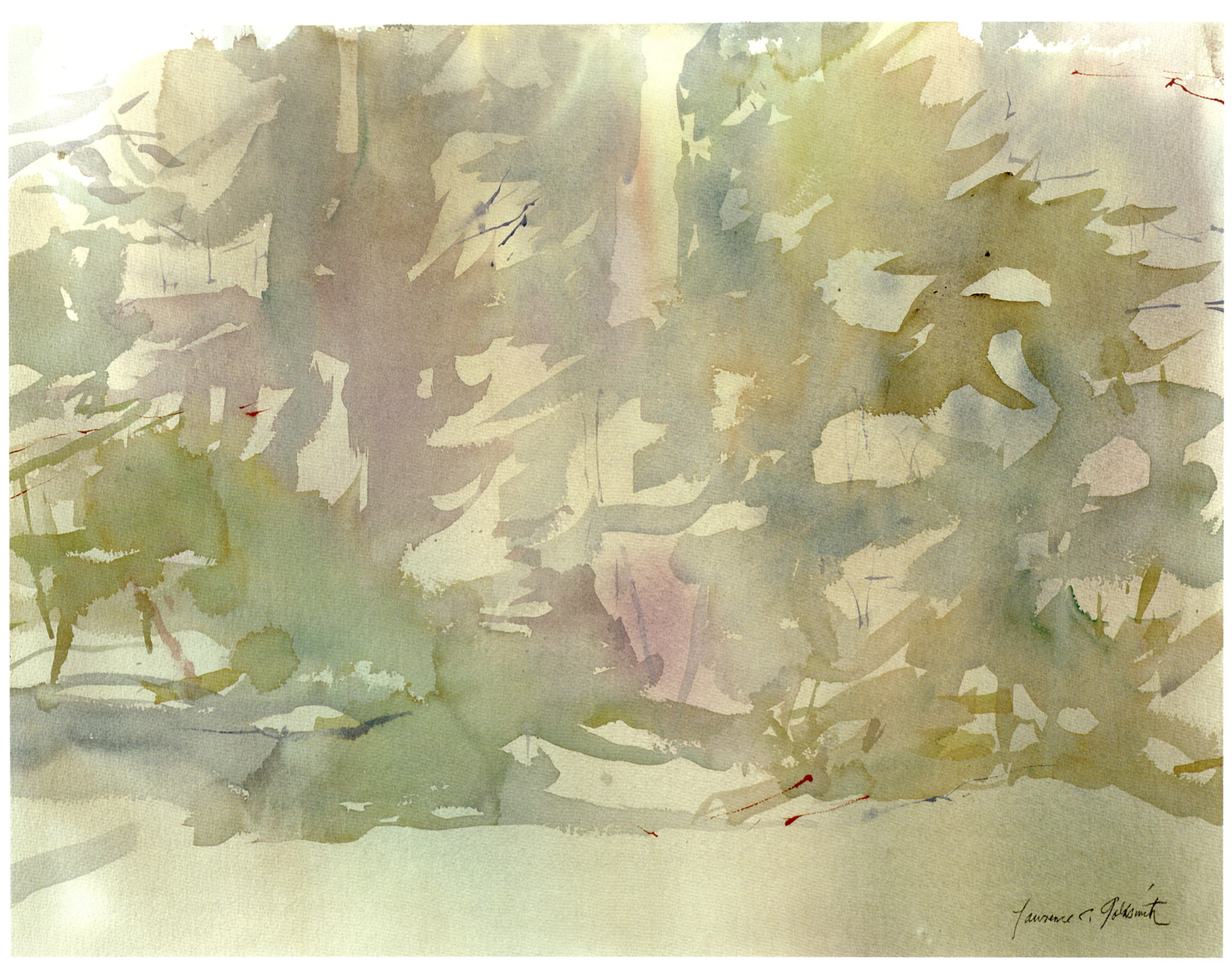

28 *Gentle Forest*, 1995. There is a beauty in delicacy that is sometimes overlooked. Here my goal was to establish the mood as gently as possible.

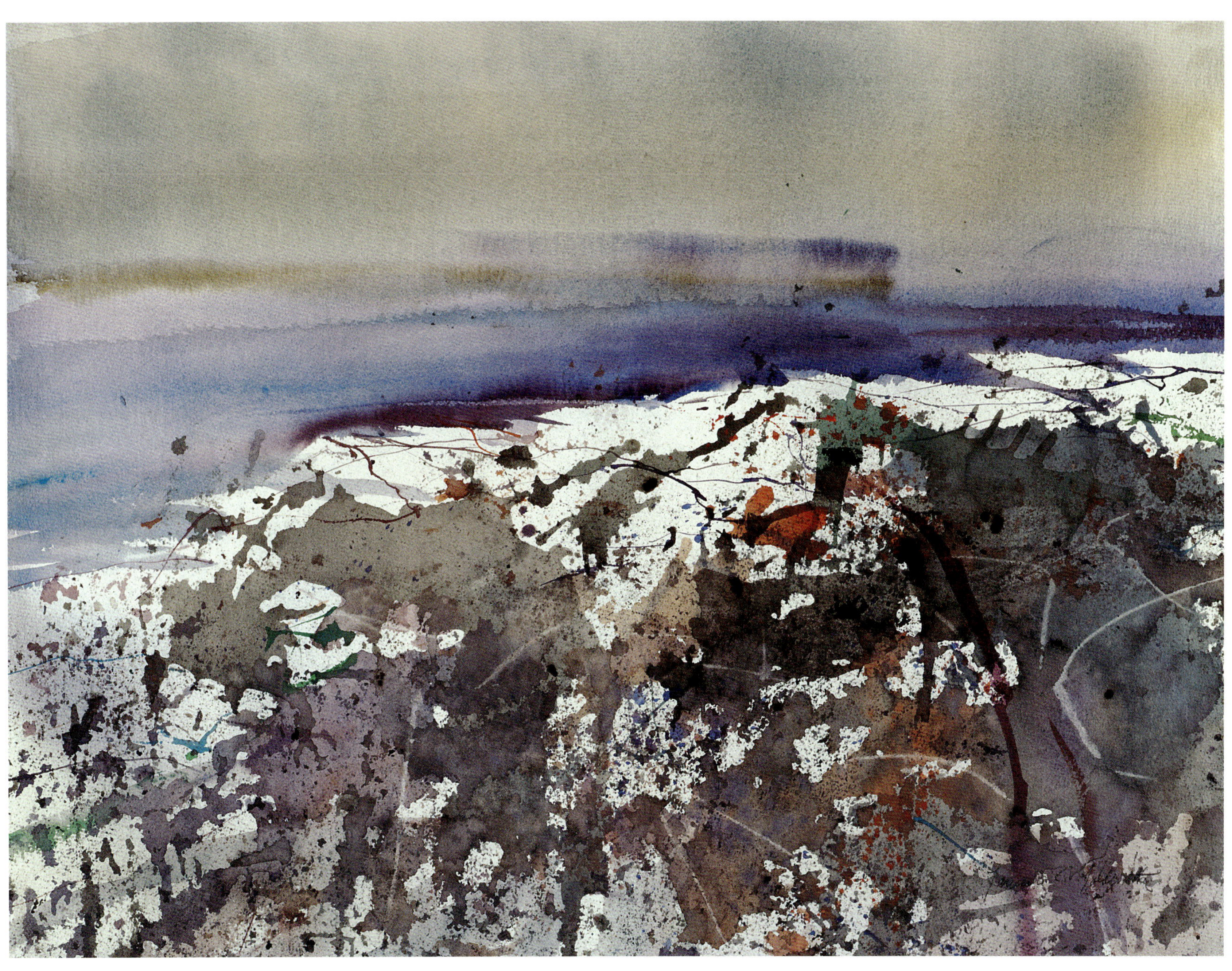

29 *So Many Rocks,* 1997. A weary visitor whose husband had just achieved his ambition of visiting Monhegan complained, “Too many artists. Too many rocks.” This rocky island, once an ancient mountain peak, provides an endless array of textured and wrinkled surfaces to inspire all those artists.

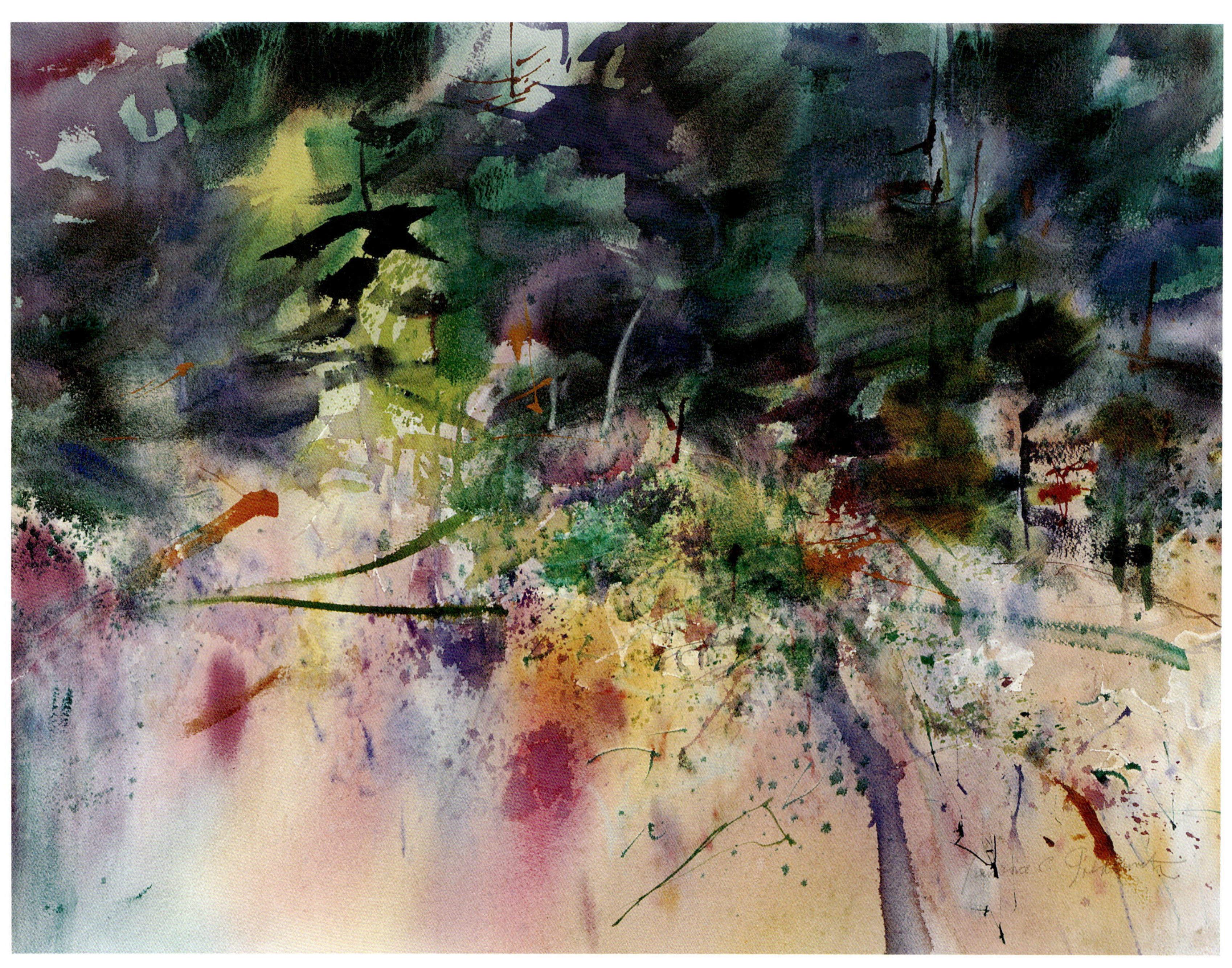

30 *Here and Now,* 1997. The lush, deep color becomes more important than the forest. One might even imagine the sea replacing forest here.

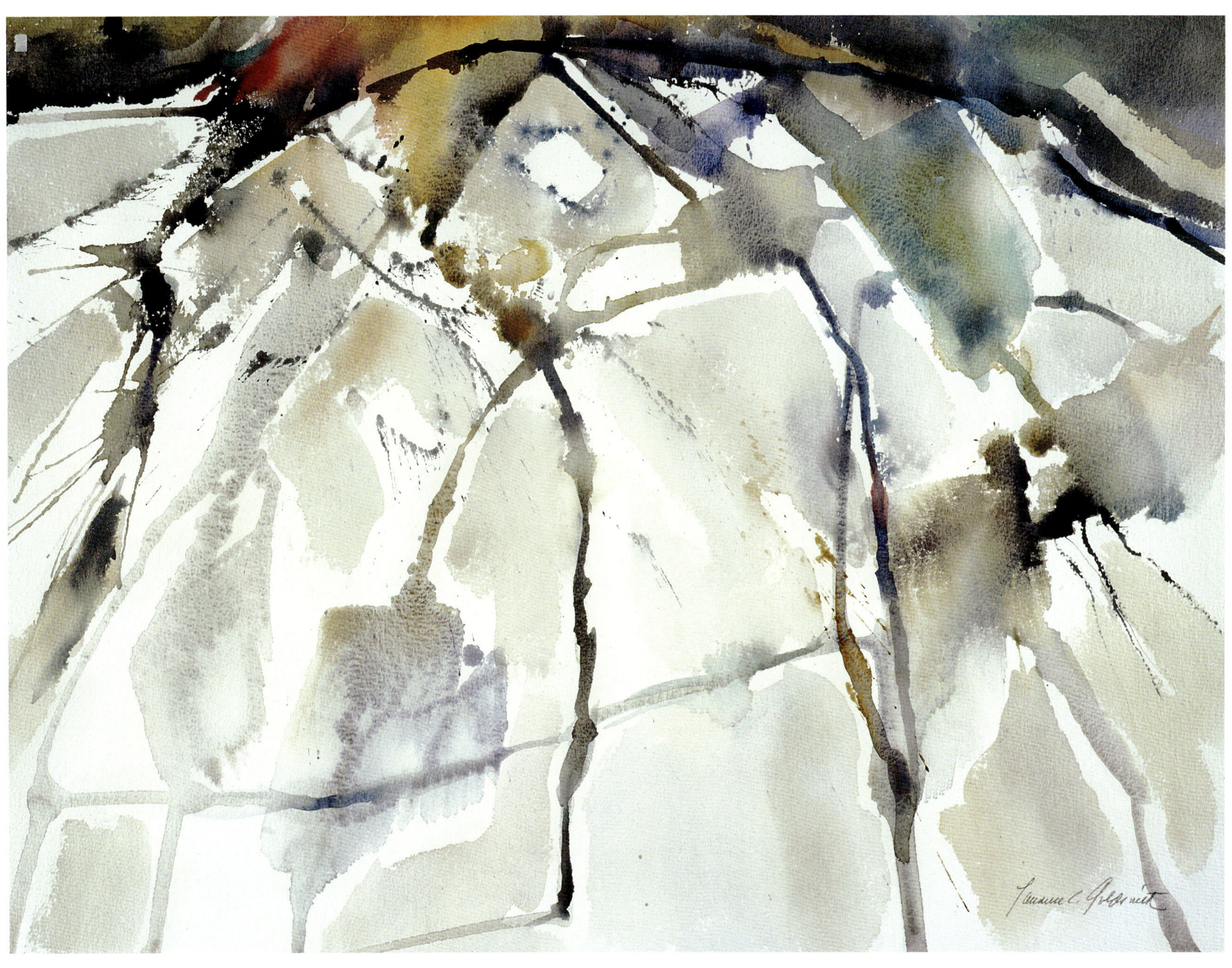

31 *Rocky Command*, 1998.

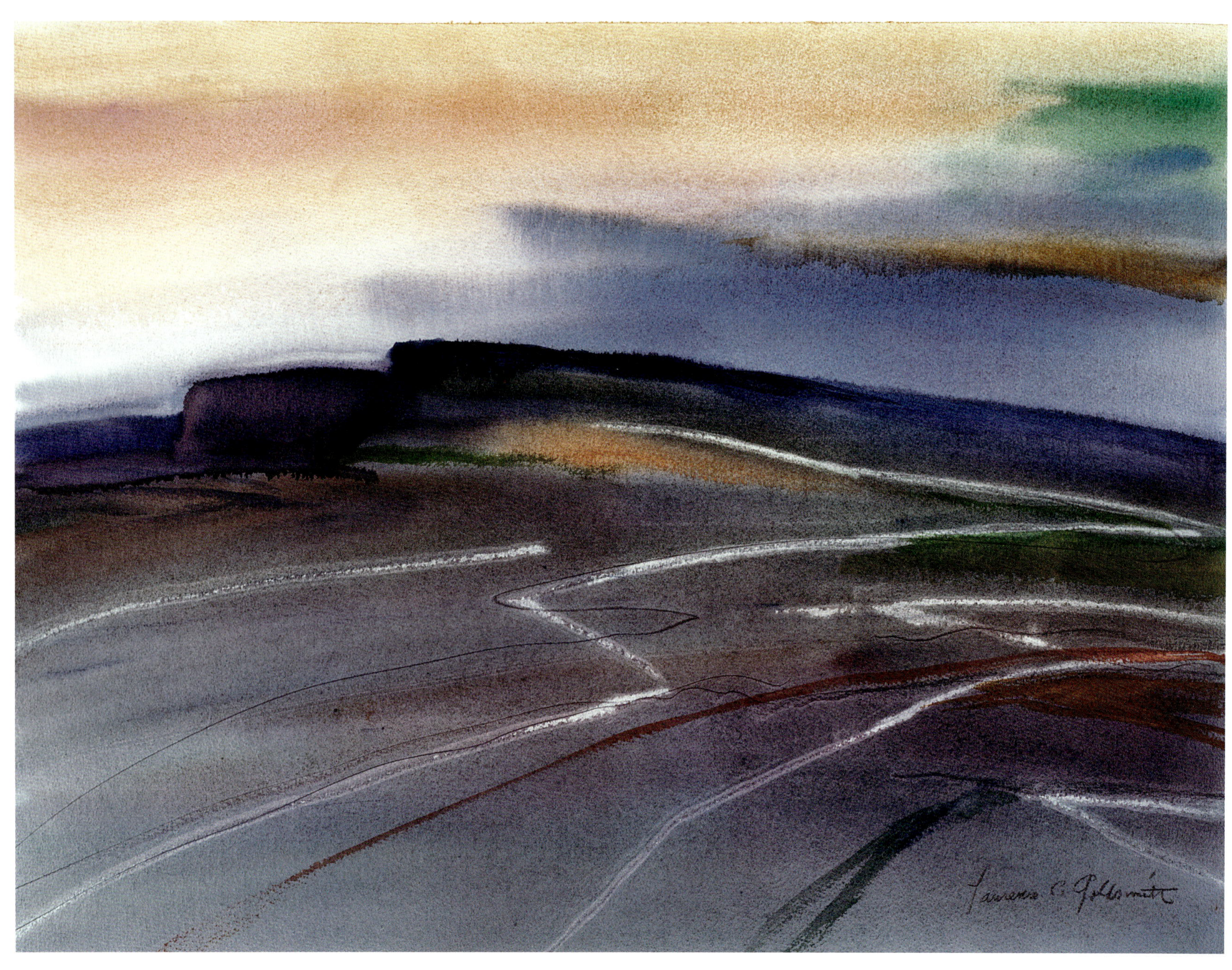

32 *High and Mighty*, 1998.

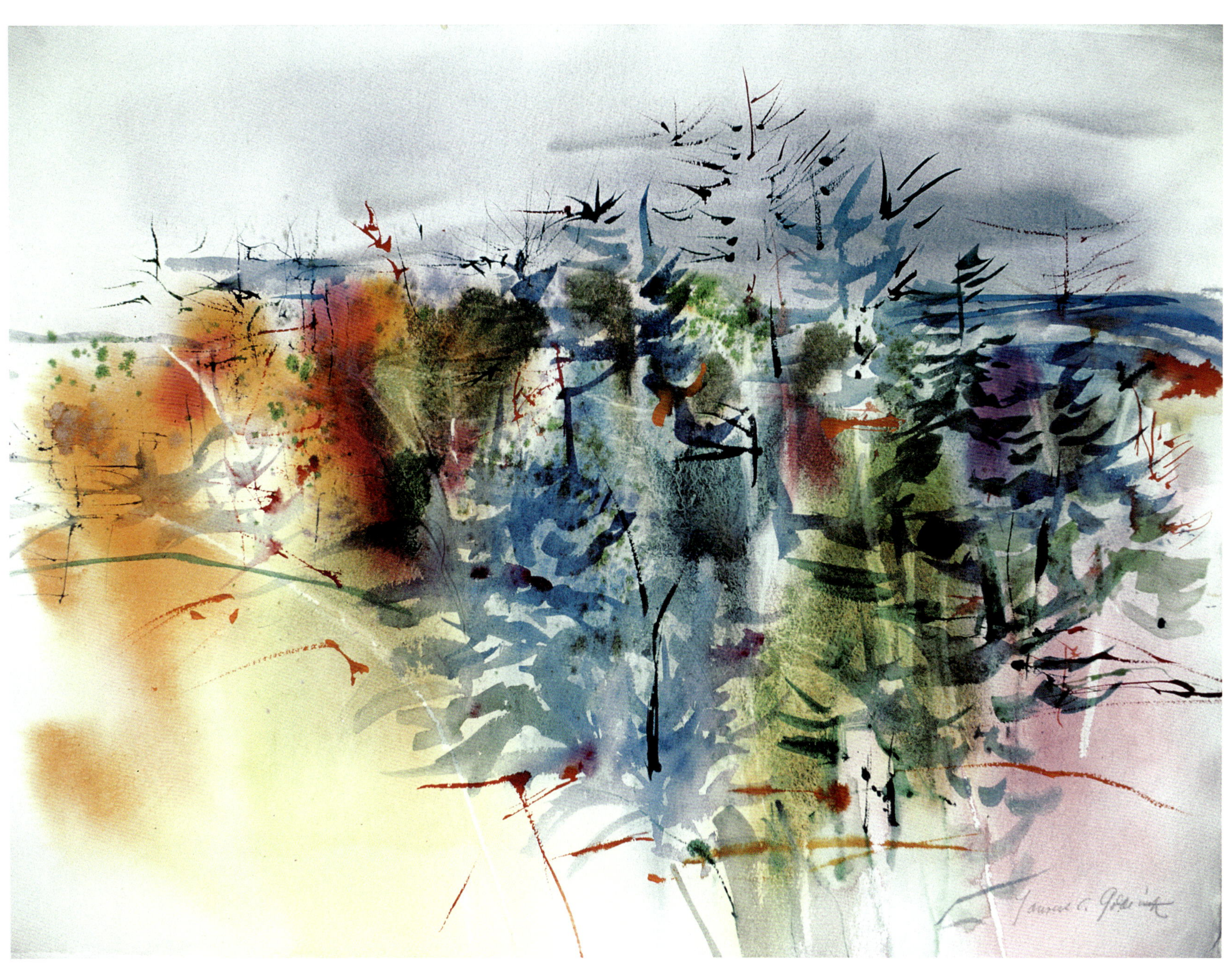

33 *Dreamcatcher Hour,* 1998. Collection of Monhegan Art Museum.

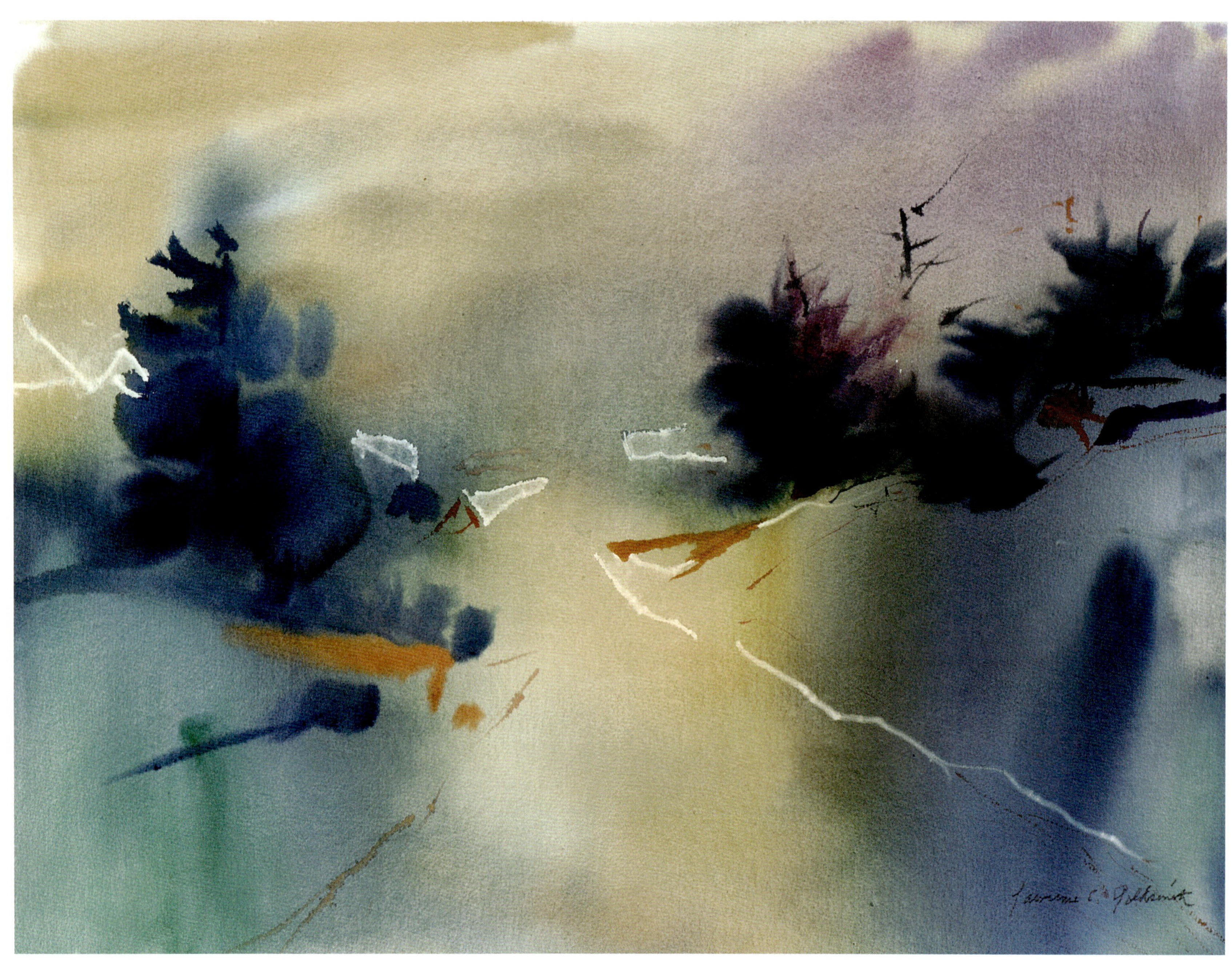

34 *Fog Mystique,* 2000. In and out of the forest, the layers of paint are confined to two or three to maintain the lightness of fog.

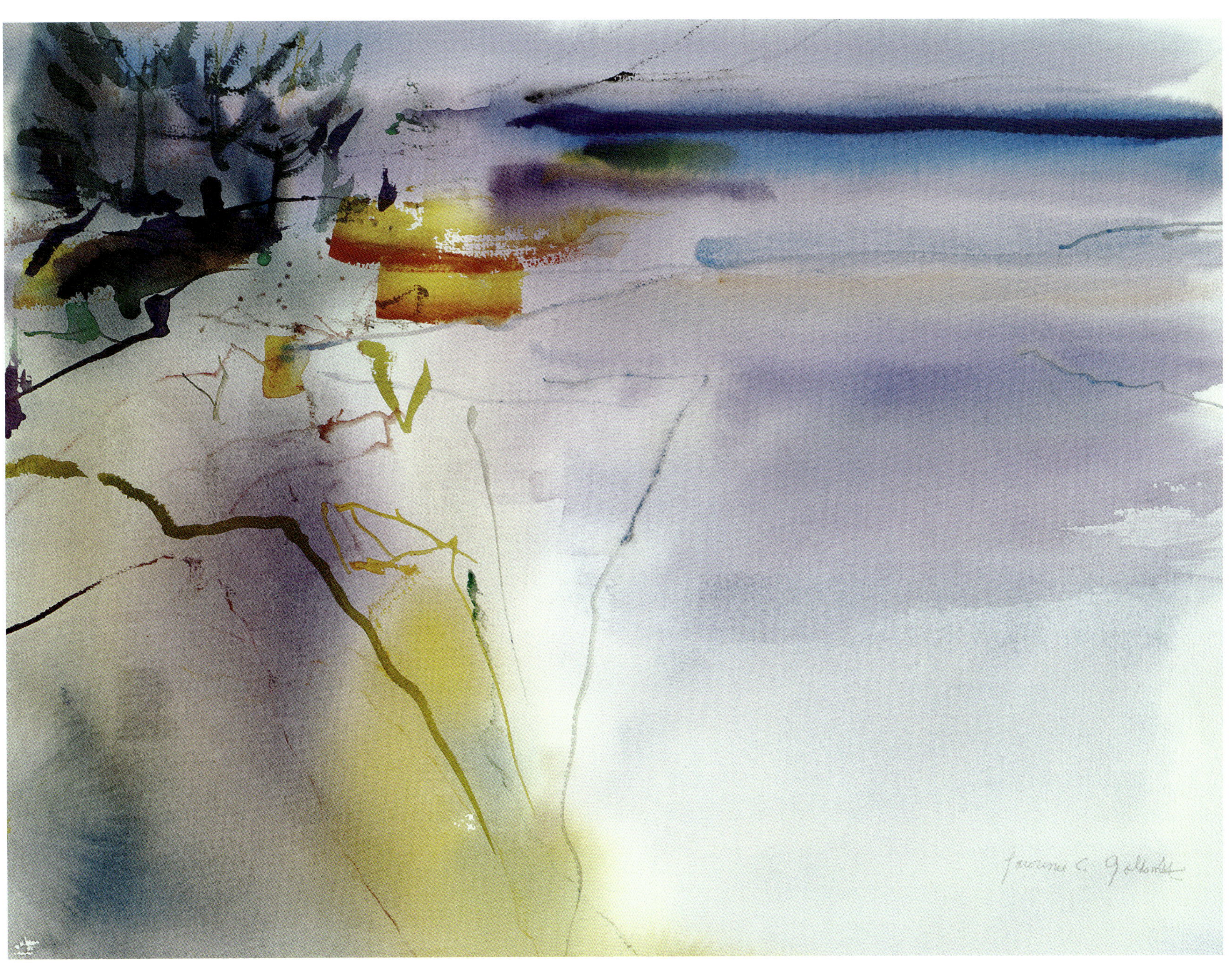

35 *Seaward*, 2002.

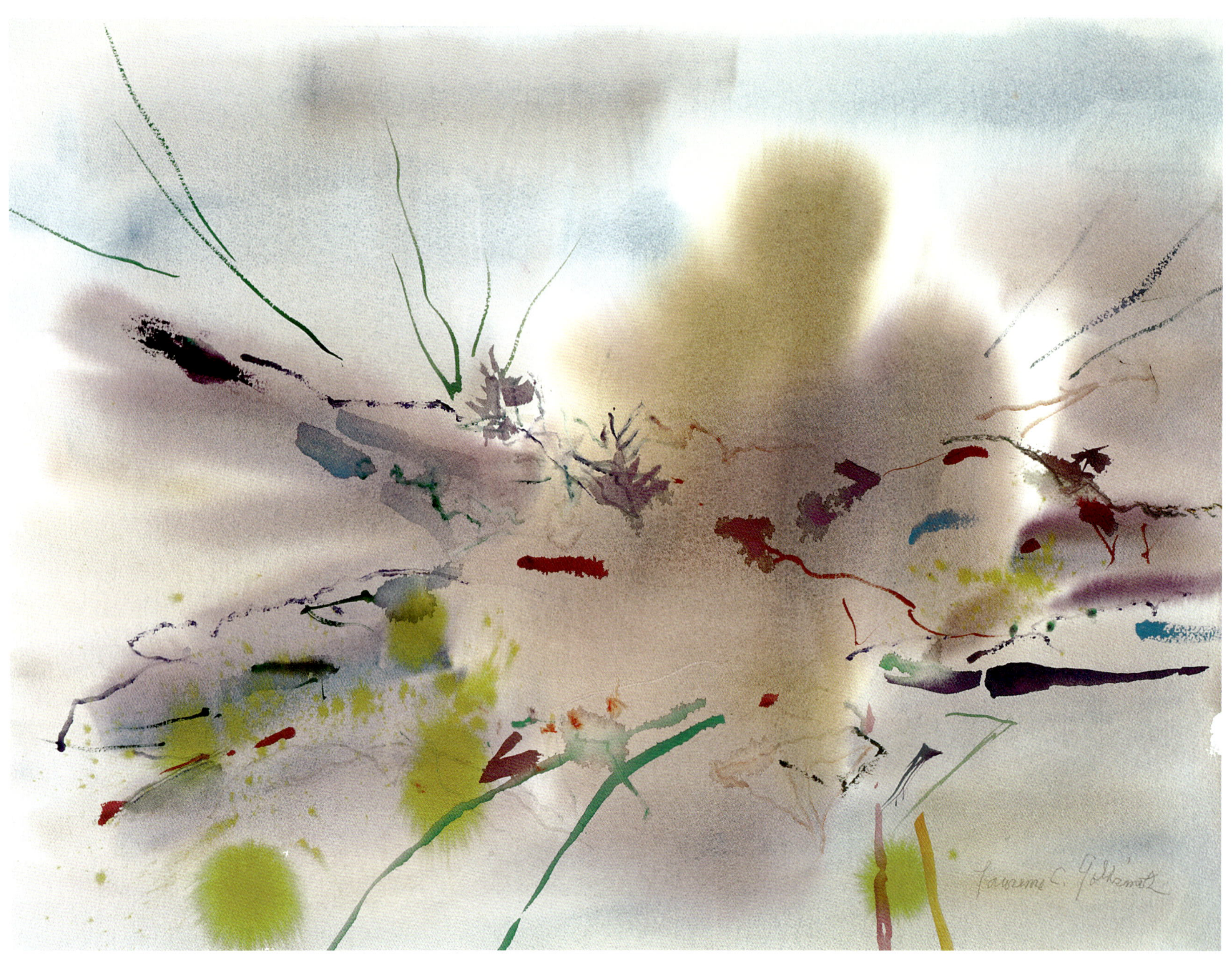

36 *Islandia in Soft Light,* 2002. One of a series, this painting of soft light carries with it a fictional quality, a creation of my imagination.

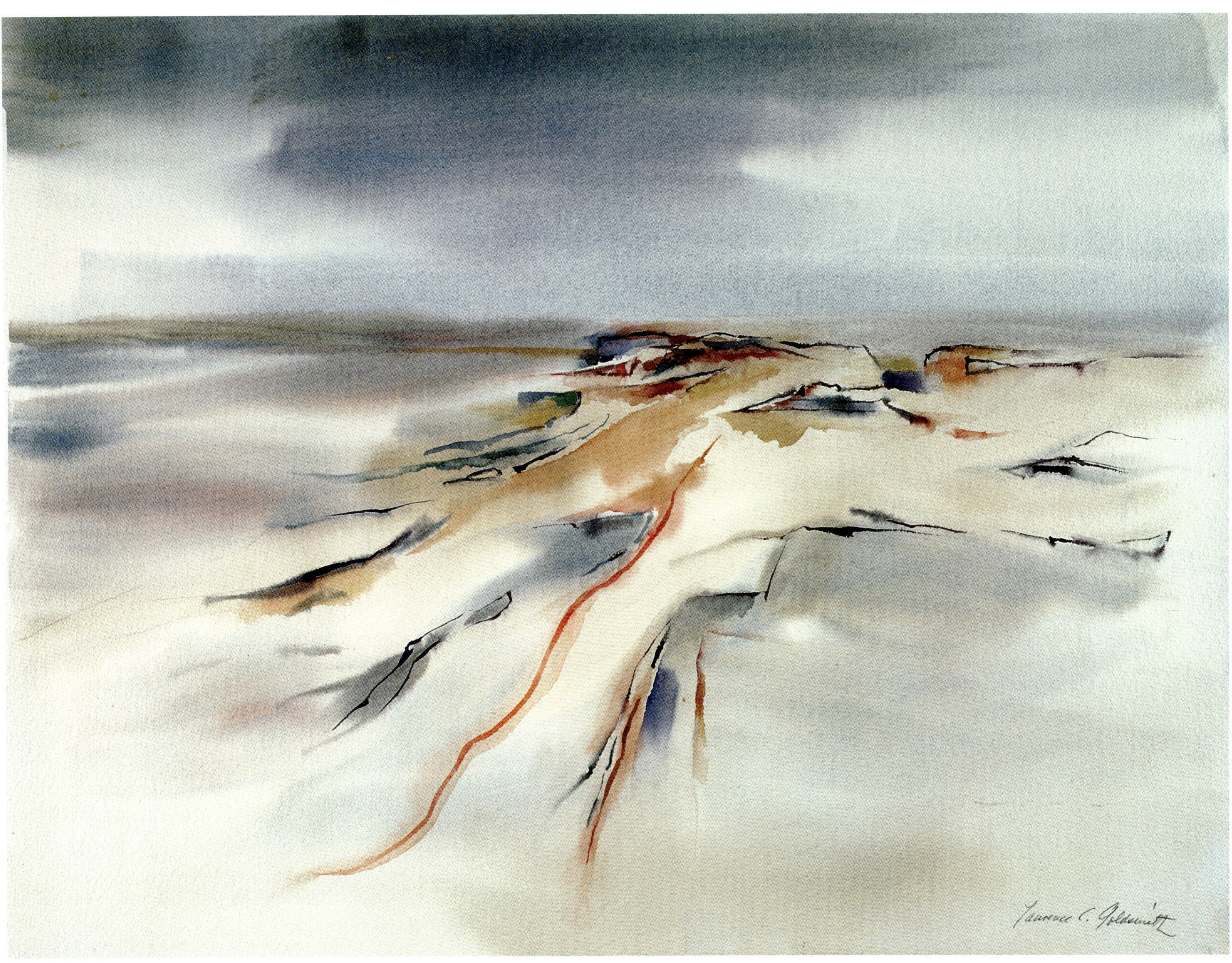

37 *Lonely Headlands,* 1986. Monhegan headlands must get as many emotional responses as they get visitors. But a feeling of remoteness and isolation, welcome or not, is surely a common reaction.

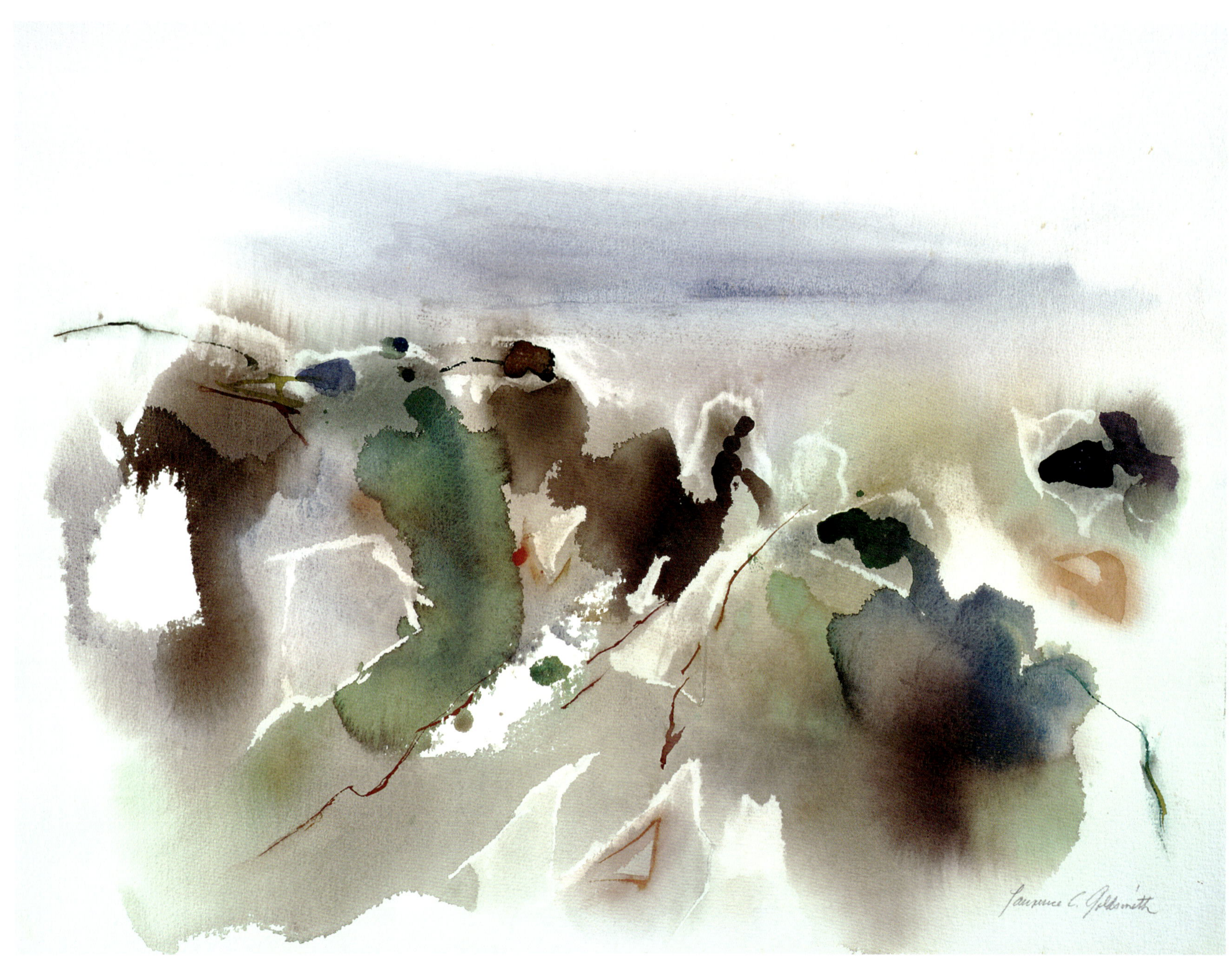

38 *Tidal Gestures,* 1986.

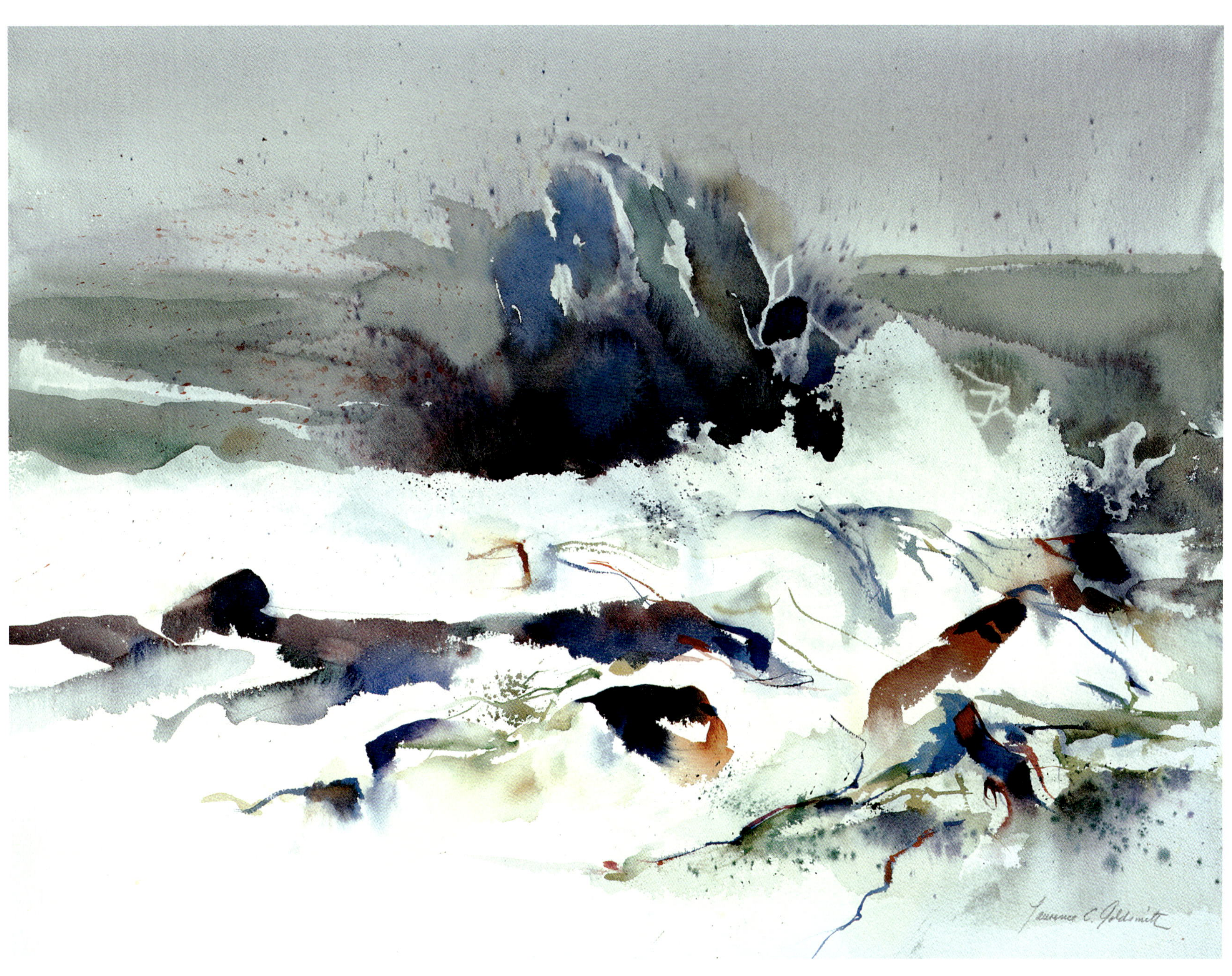

39 *Saltwater Might,* 1987. Like most painters of the sea, I revel in the power of the surf.

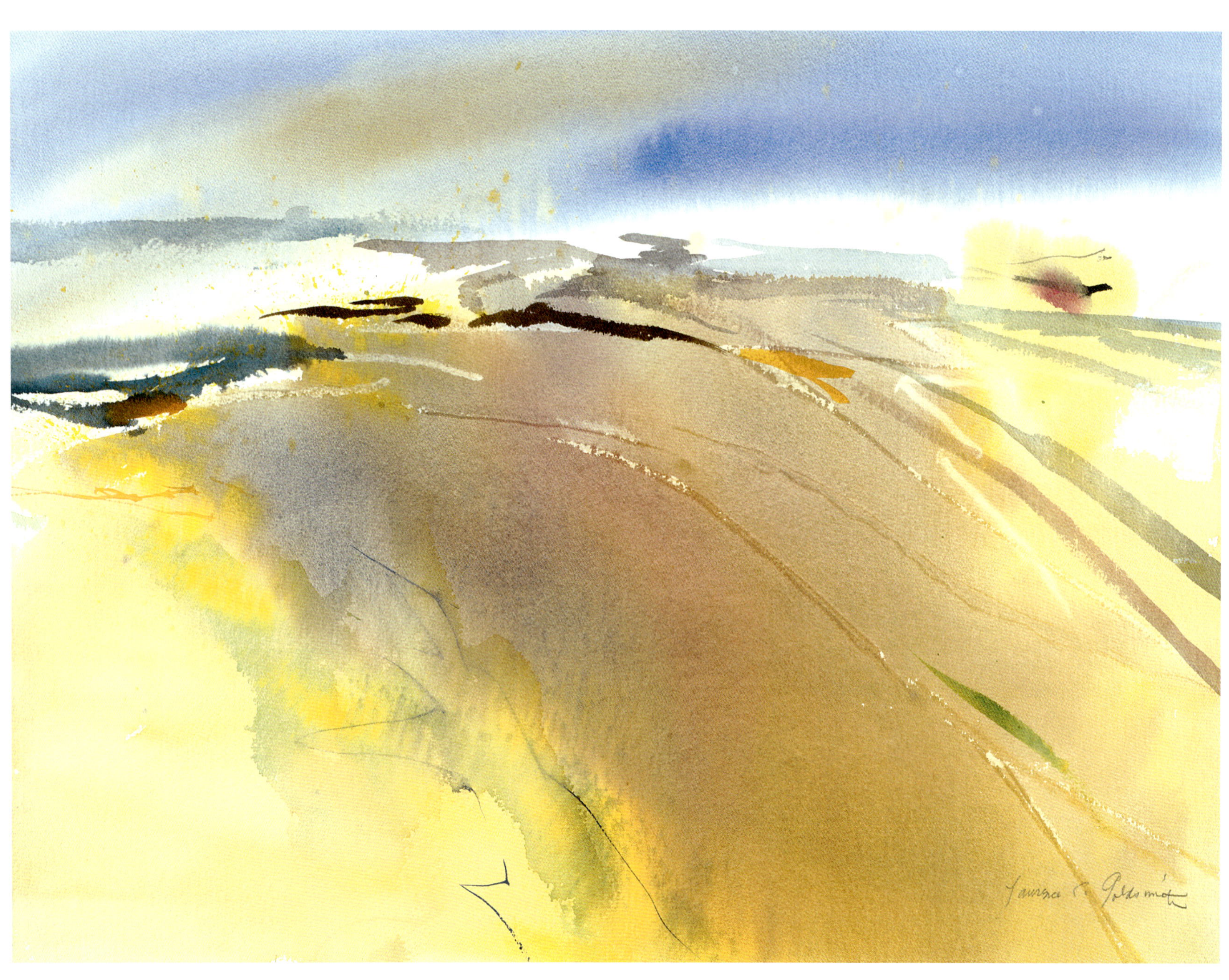

40 *Shoreline*, 1990. A Bailey Island (Maine) beach.

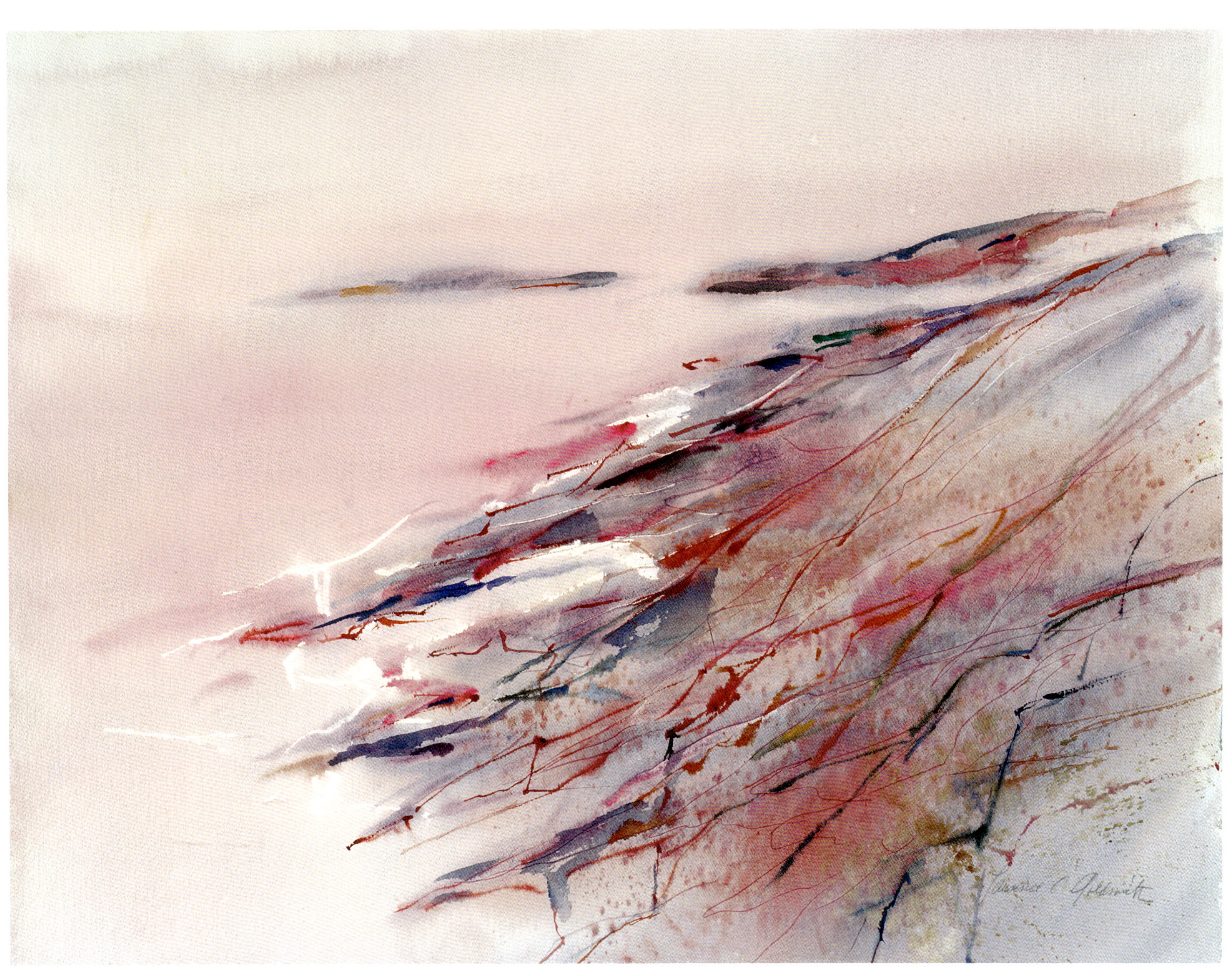

41 *Early Light,* 1991. Rose-colored air promising warmth at the dawn of a summer day.

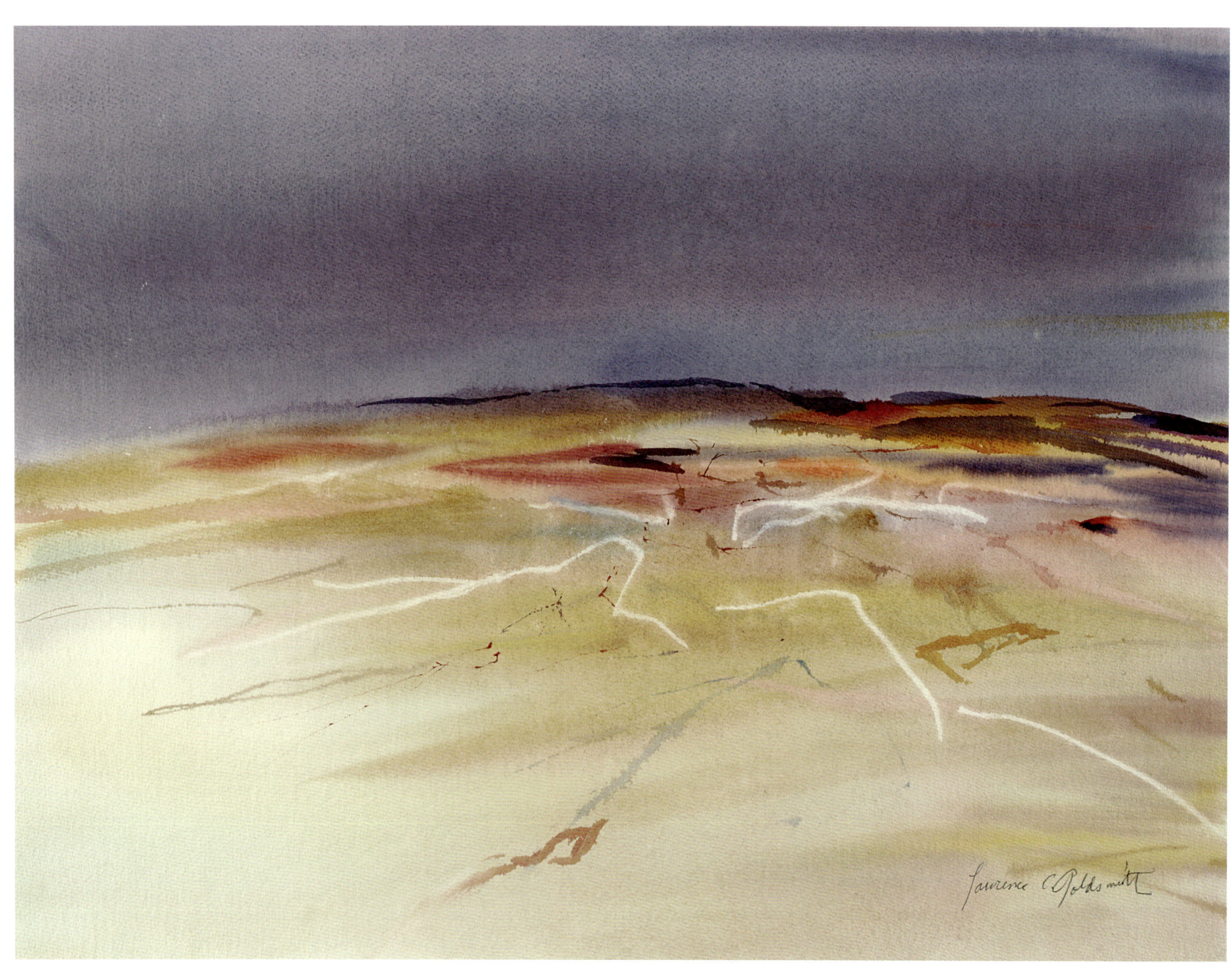

42 *Seven O'Clock*, 1995. Time makes its own mood.

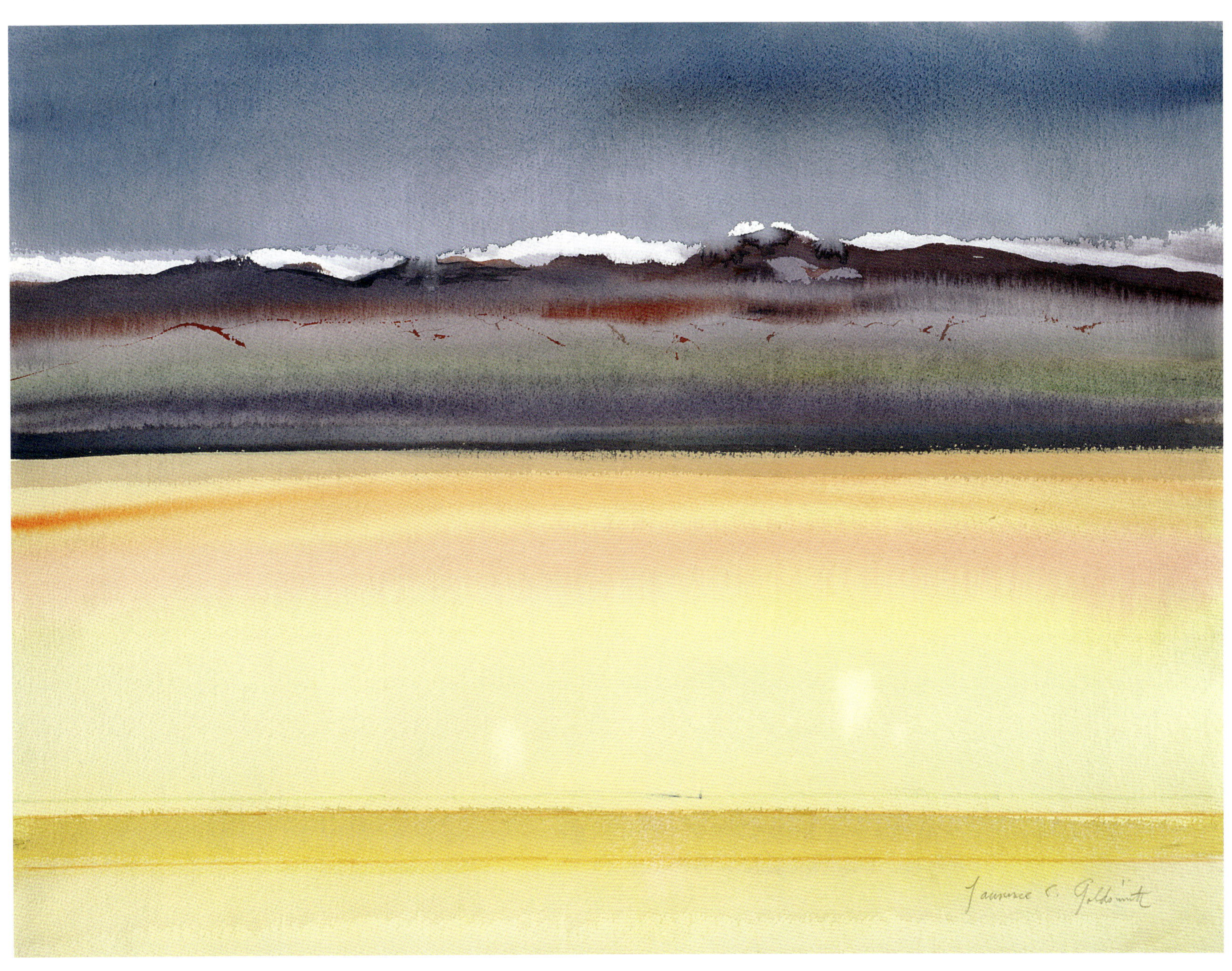

43 *Saltwater Facade,* 1996. Private collection.

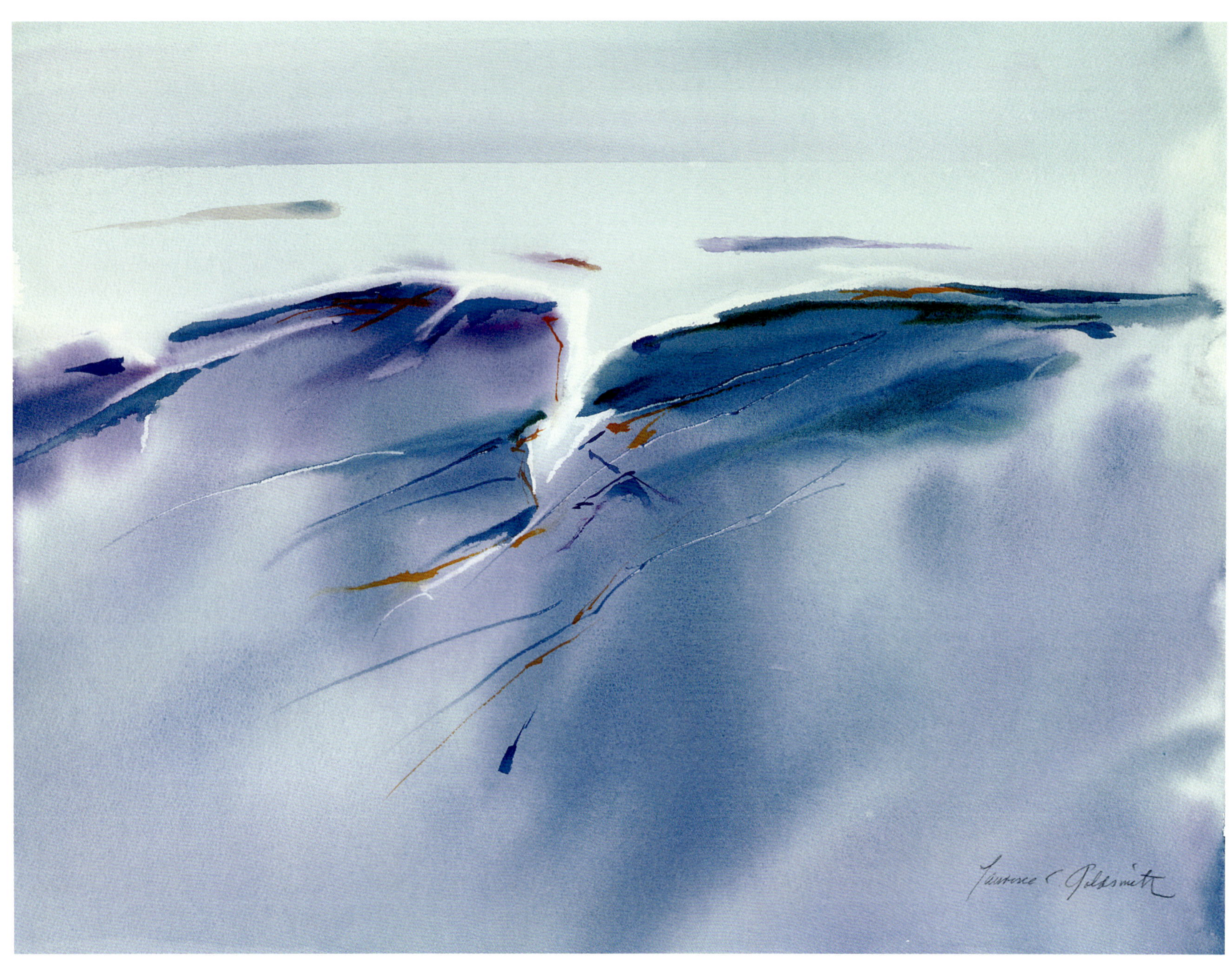

44 *North by Northeast XXXV,* 1997. From a series based on collected impressions from Maine, Nova Scotia, and Newfoundland.

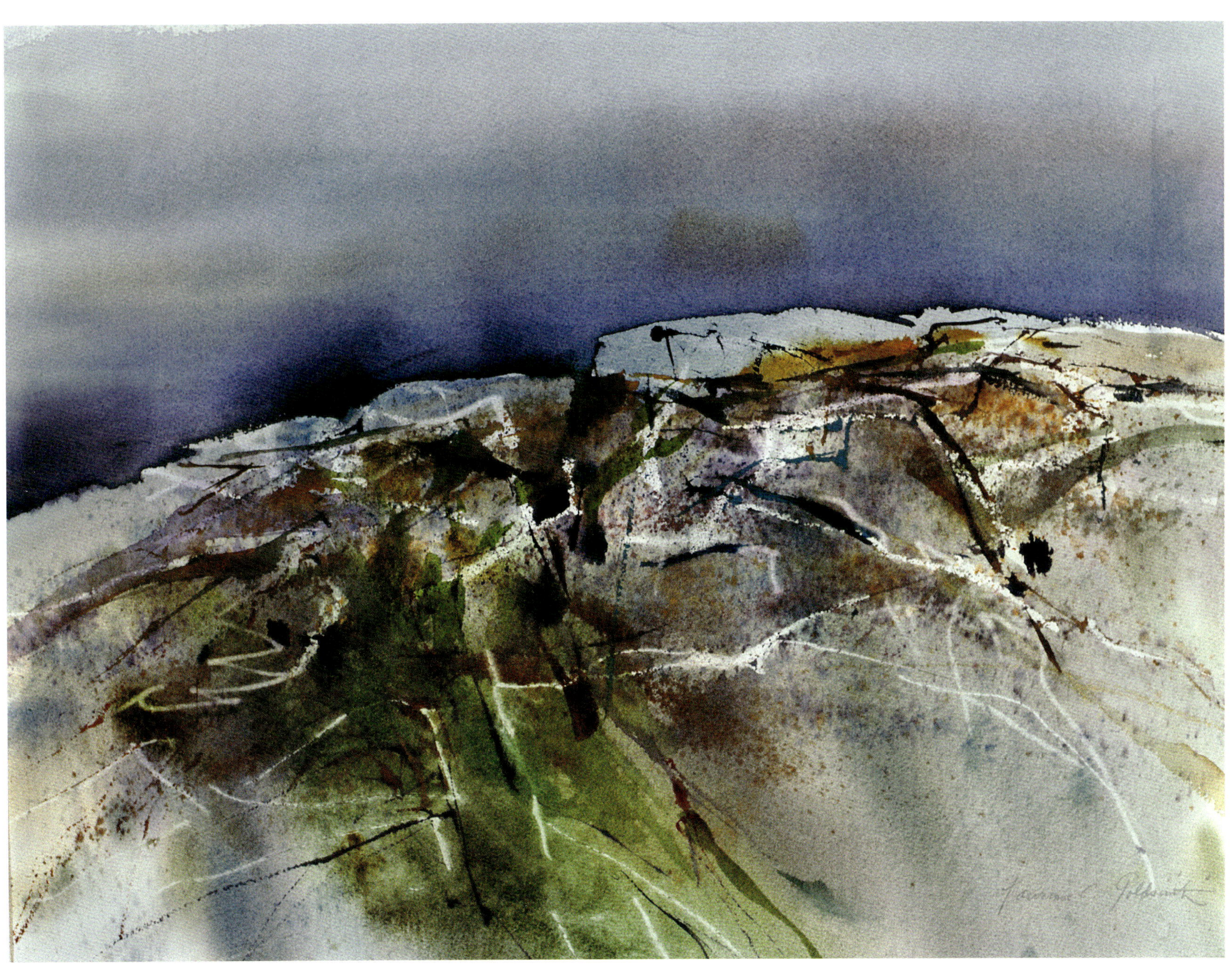

45 *Facing Rock*, 1998. Collection of Monhegan Art Museum.

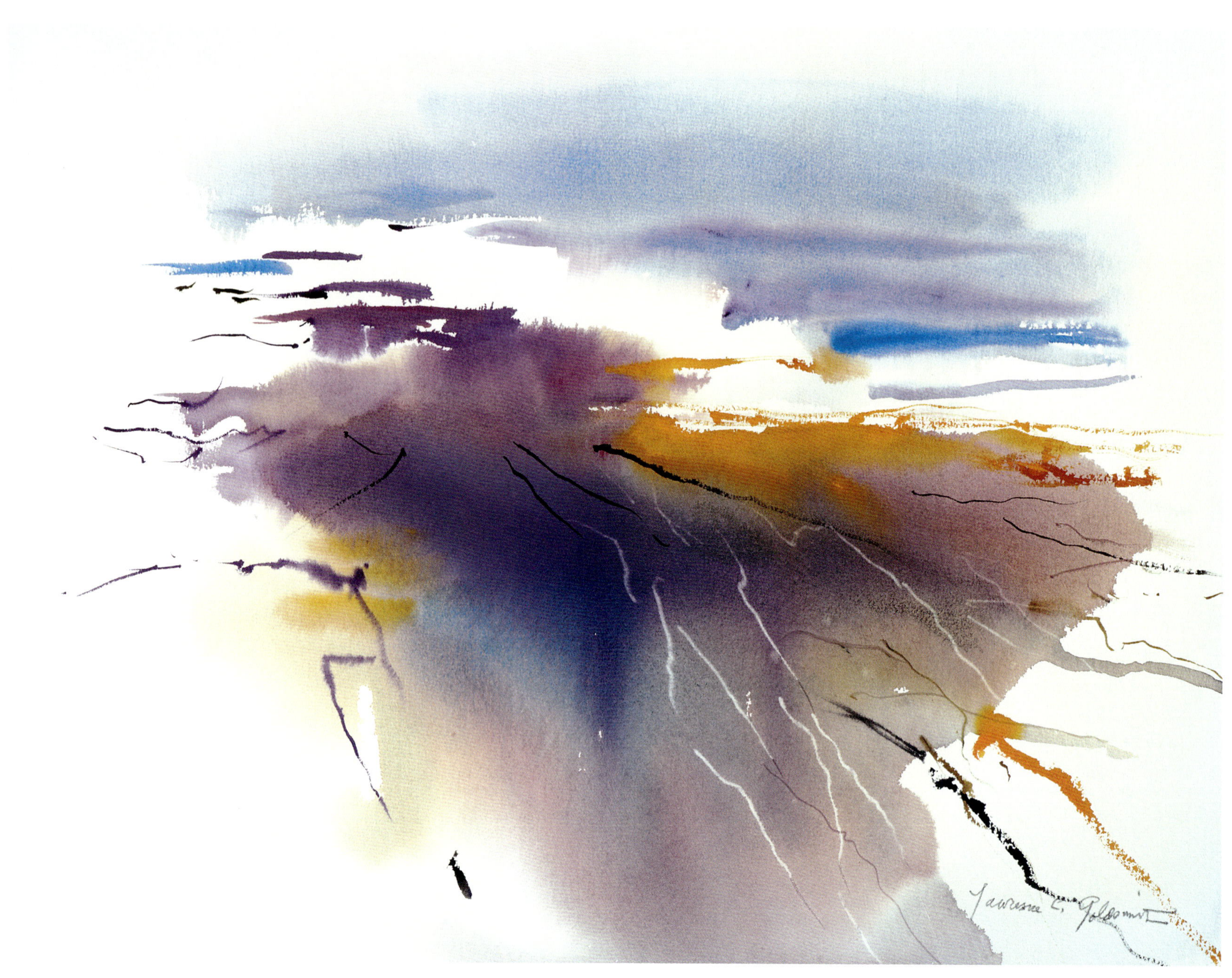

46 *White Caps*, 1998. Here the startling contrast of white paper becomes strength.

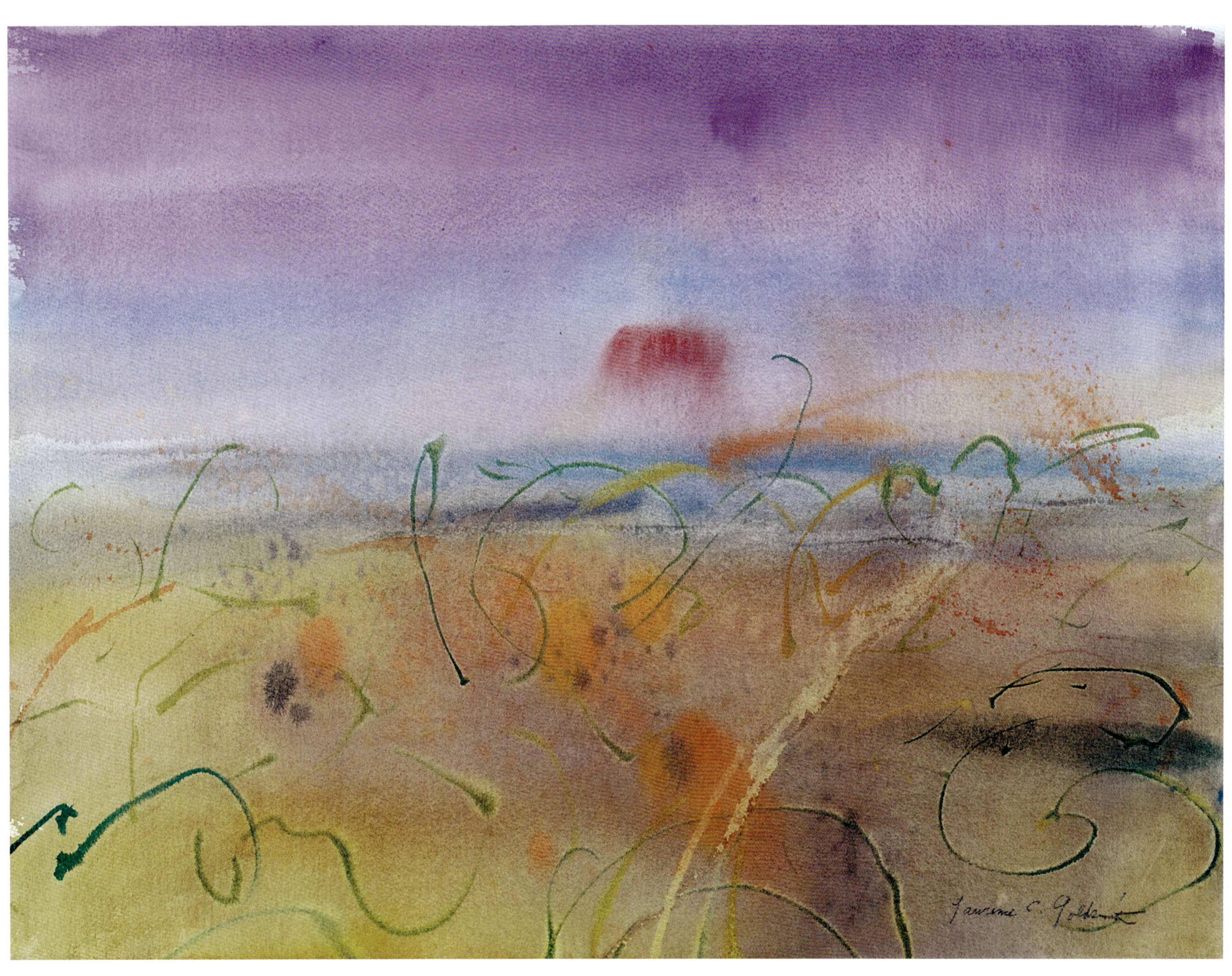

47 *Lush Stillness*, 1999.

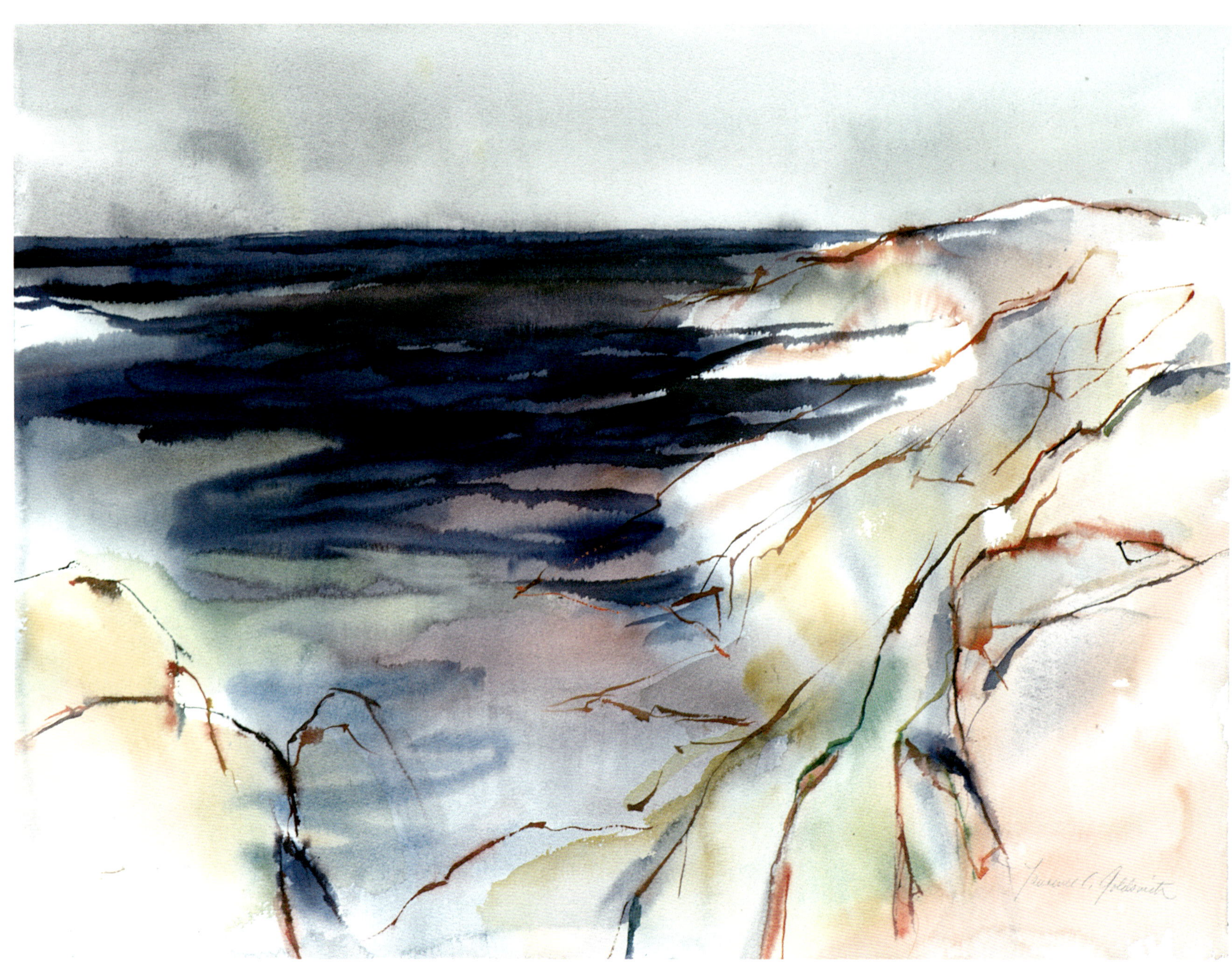

48 *Where the Sea Begins*, 2000.

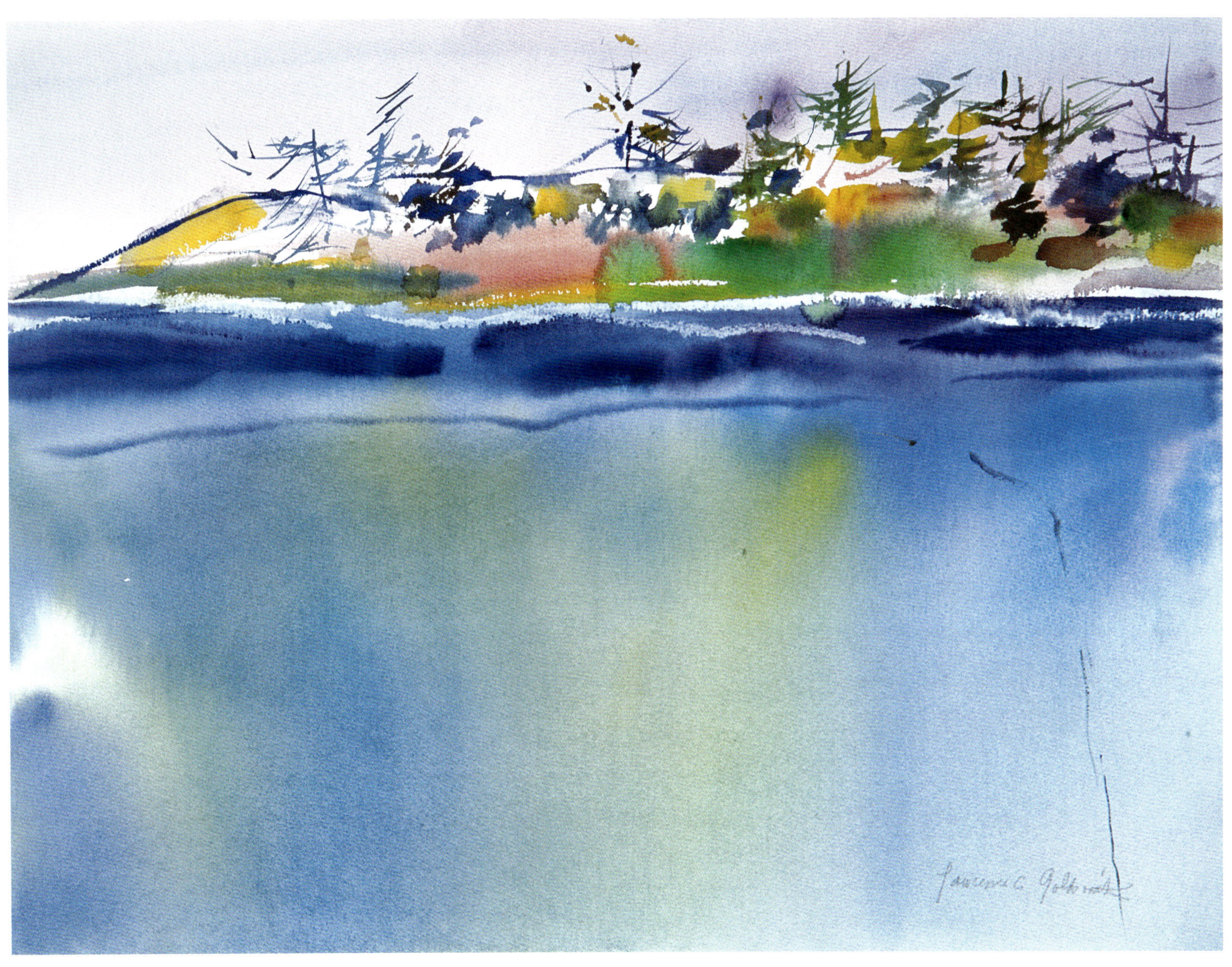

49 *Becalmed,* 2001.

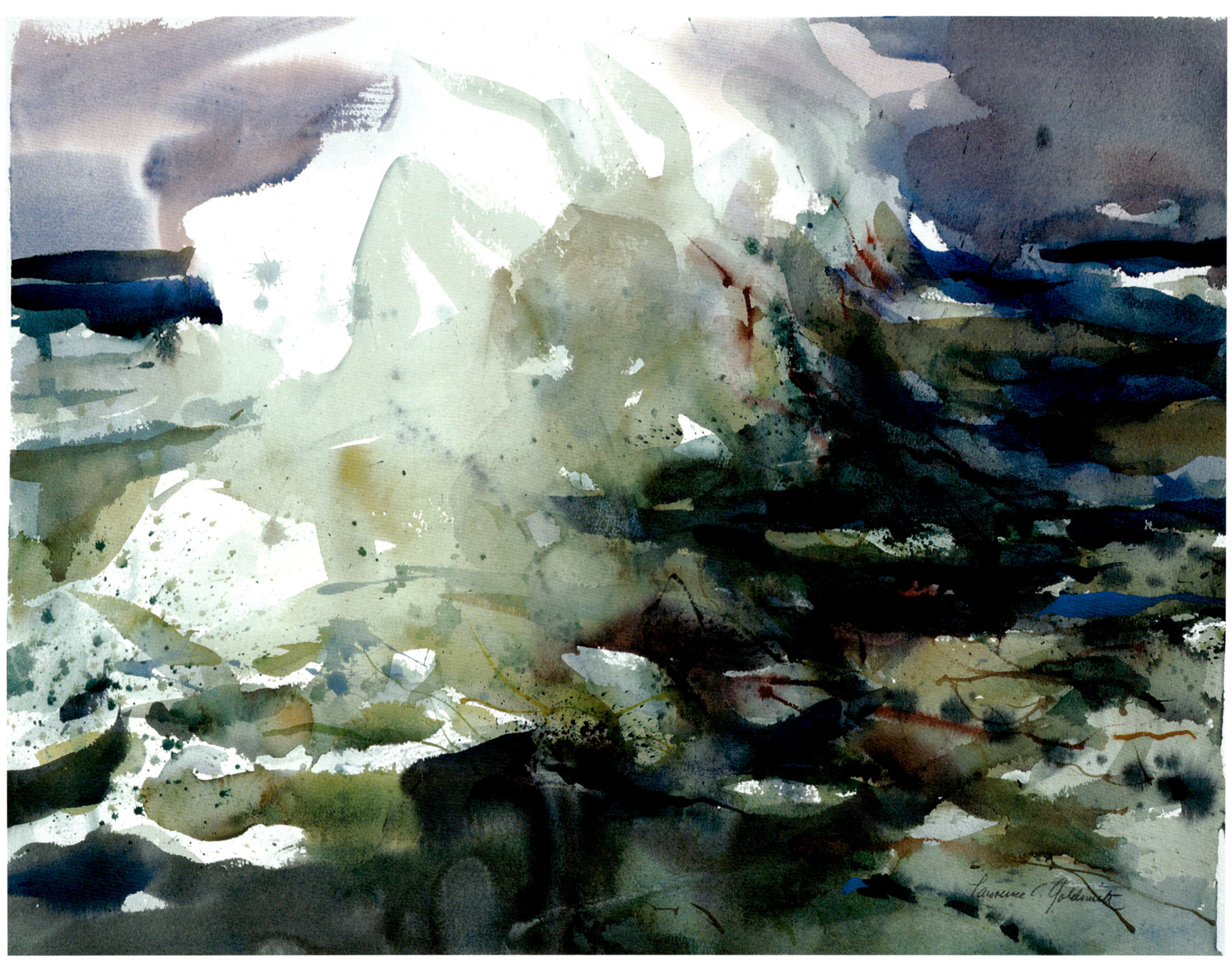

50 *Blast!*, 1988. Winslow Homer created his own storms at sea, and here I have created mine. The sea is always there to challenge the human soul.

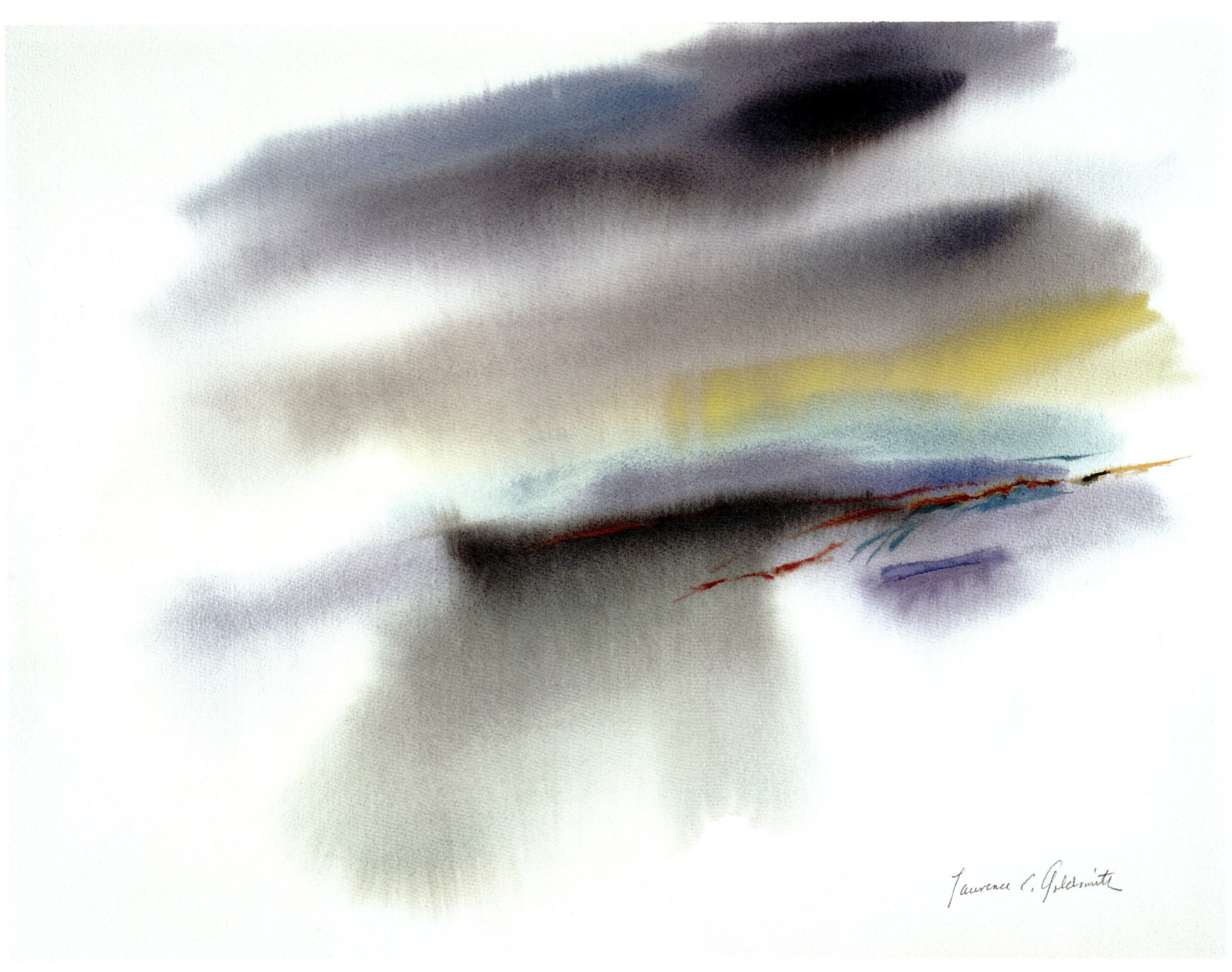

51 *Lonely Outpost,* 1989. Private collection. I use the word "lonely" so often in titles that it undoubtedly provides my productive core. True, the locations can be seen as far off and lightly inhabited, but their choice is significant. The emphasis is on the beauty of reflection and the search for inner privacy.

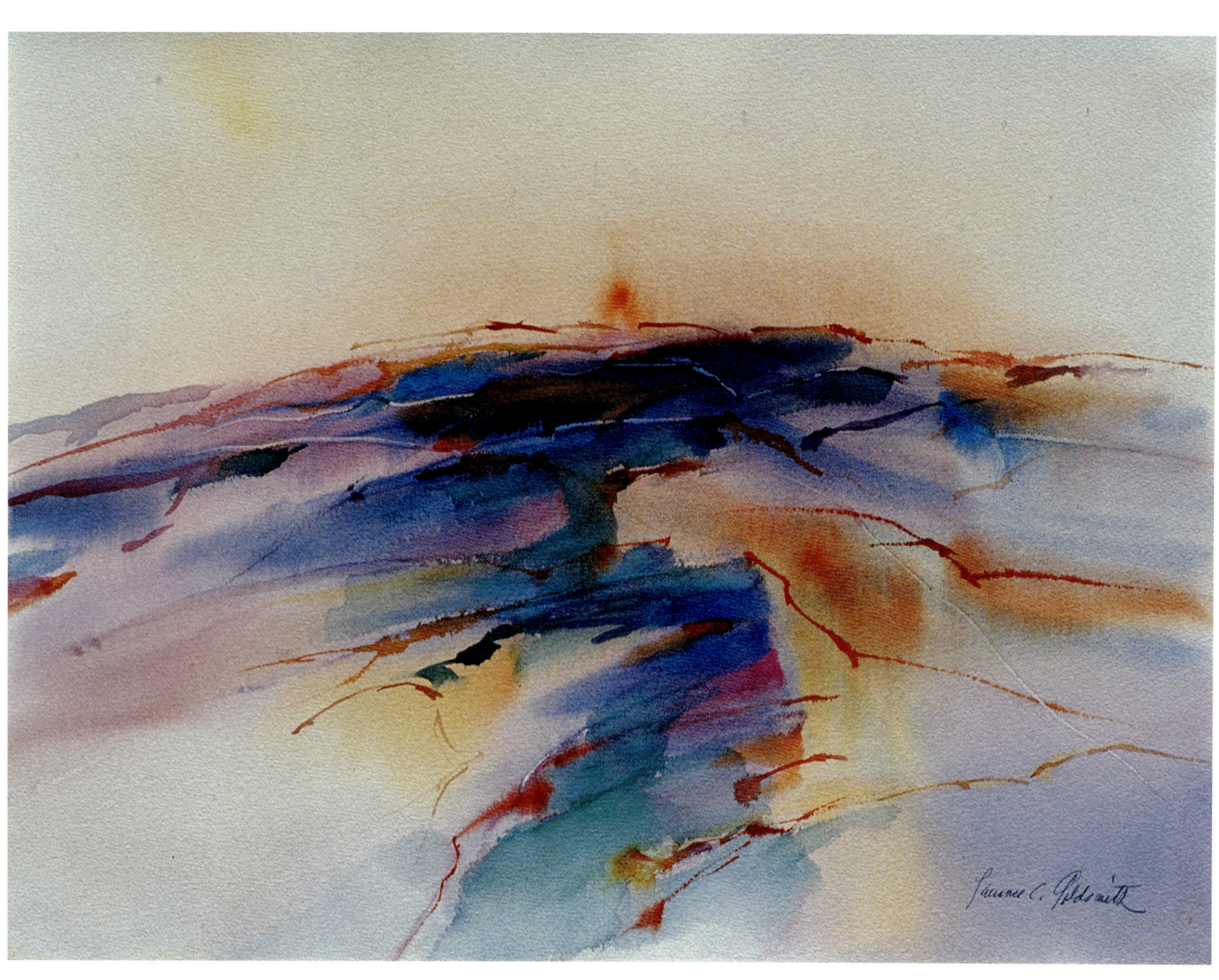

52 *Deep in Time,* 1990. Collection of Springfield Art Museum.

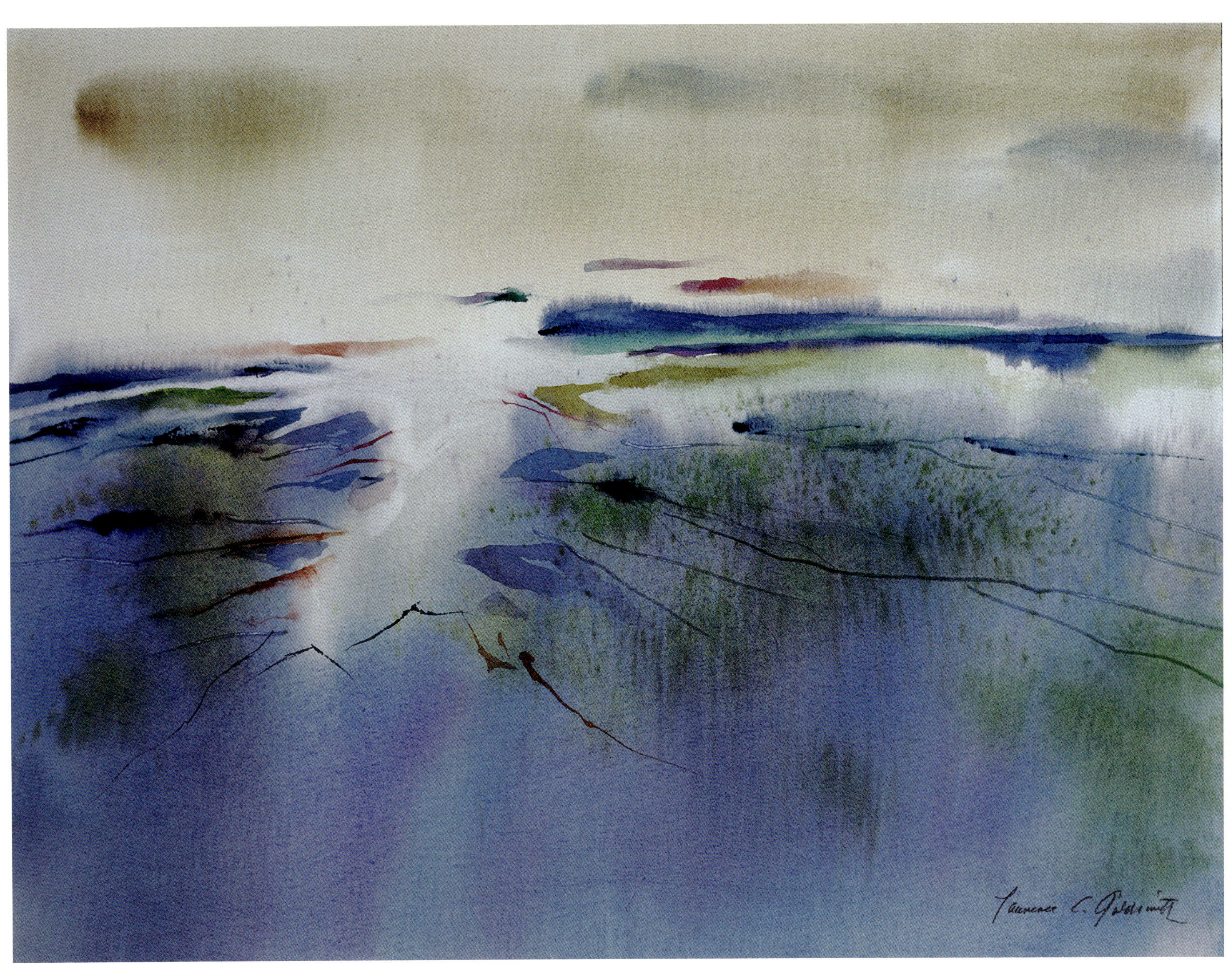

53 *North by Northeast V,* 1992. Collection of Robert Hull Fleming Museum, University of Vermont.

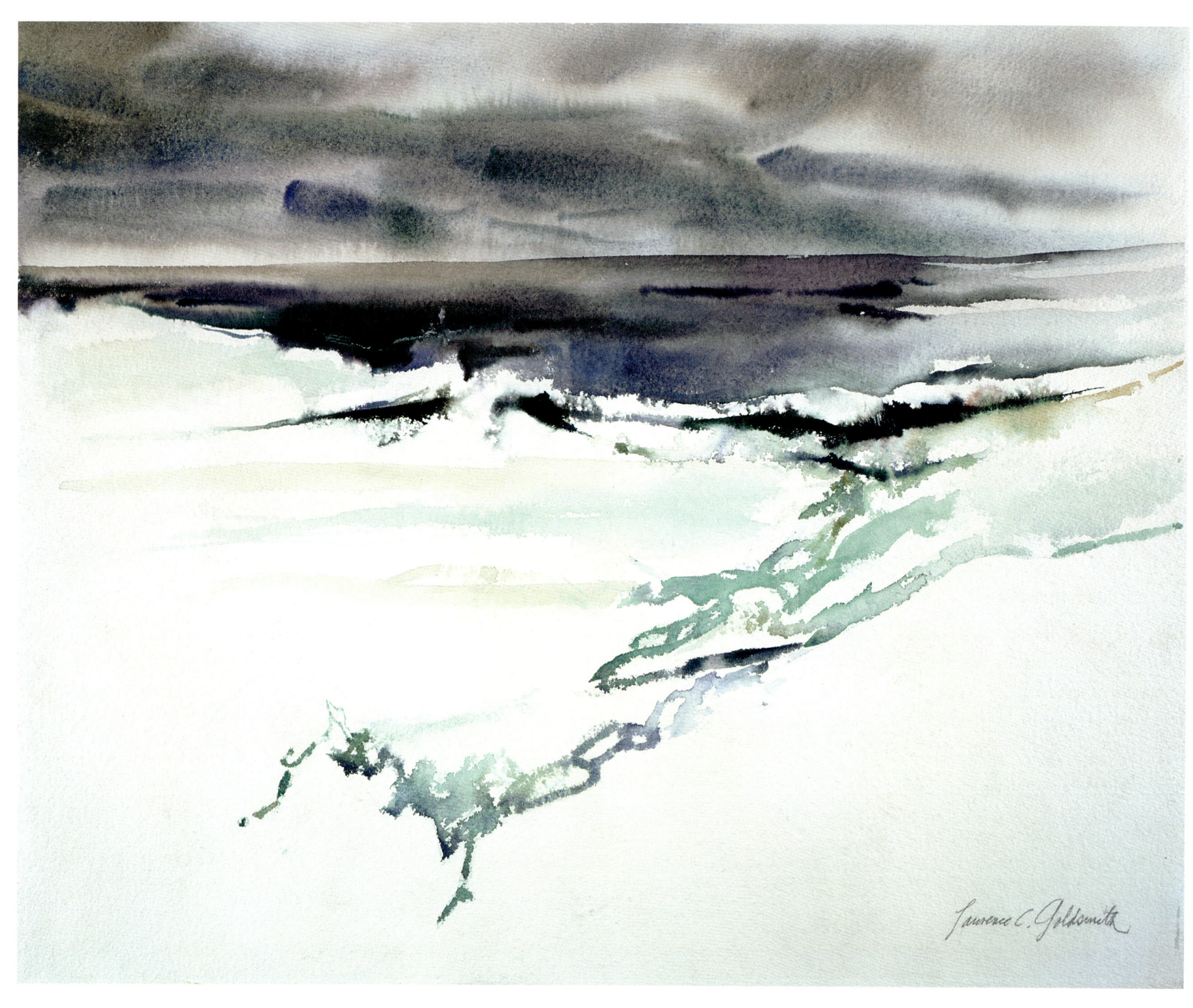

54 *Flow of Foam,* 1995, 19 x 24 in.

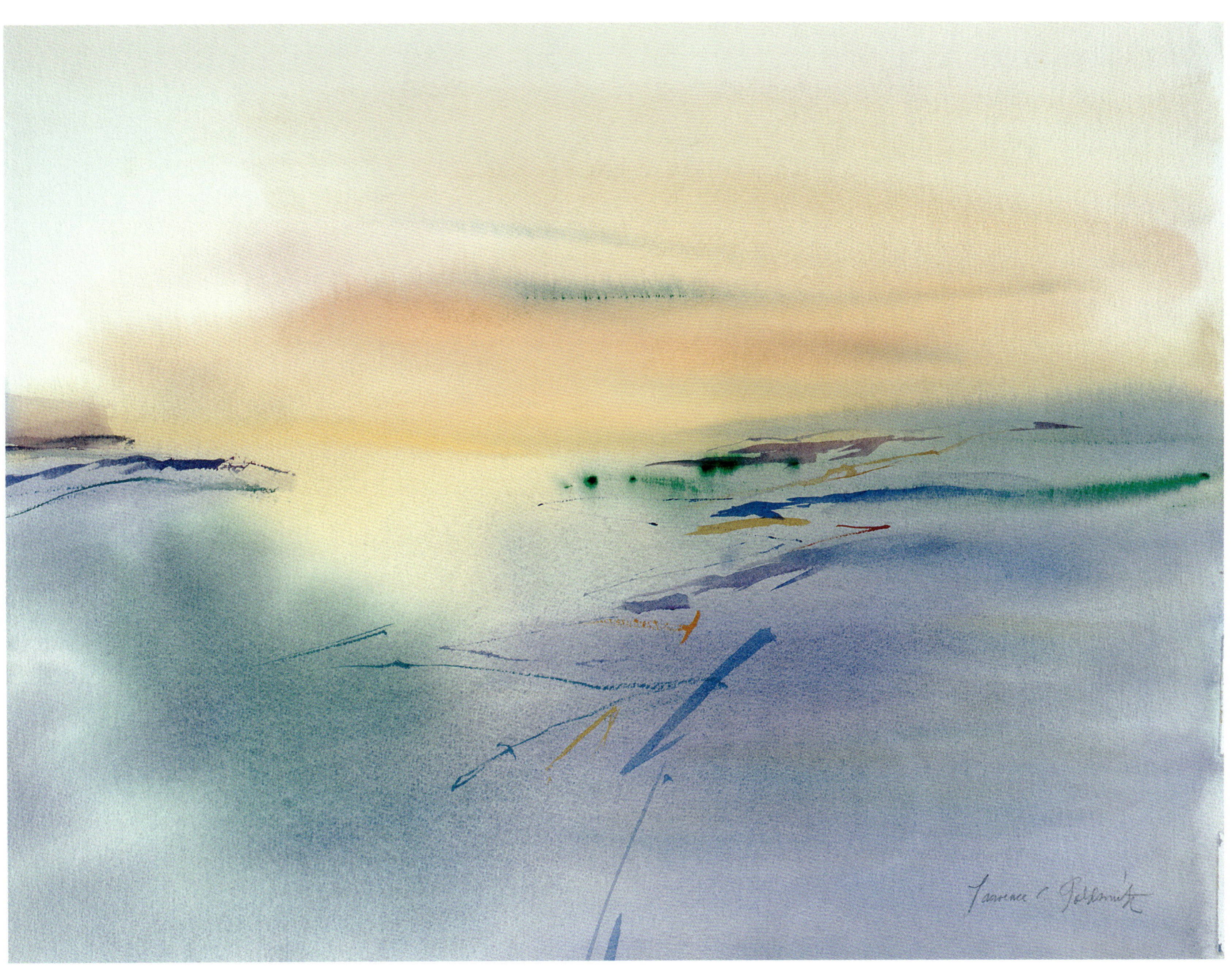

55 *Hurricane Heritage,* 1996.

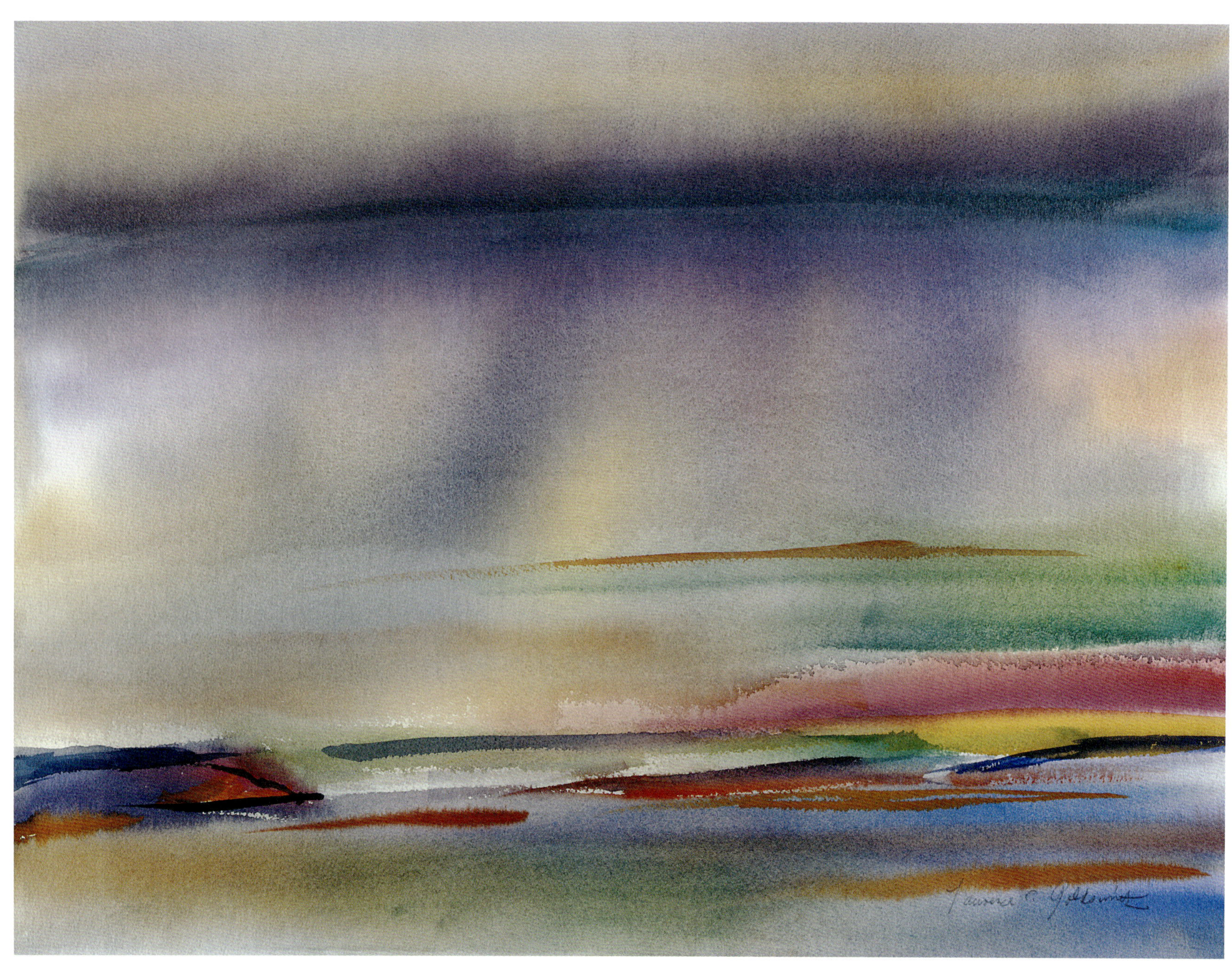

56 *Silent Harbor,* 1998. Silence can create a mood as can sound. The bands of still water form a rather abstract horizontal composition.

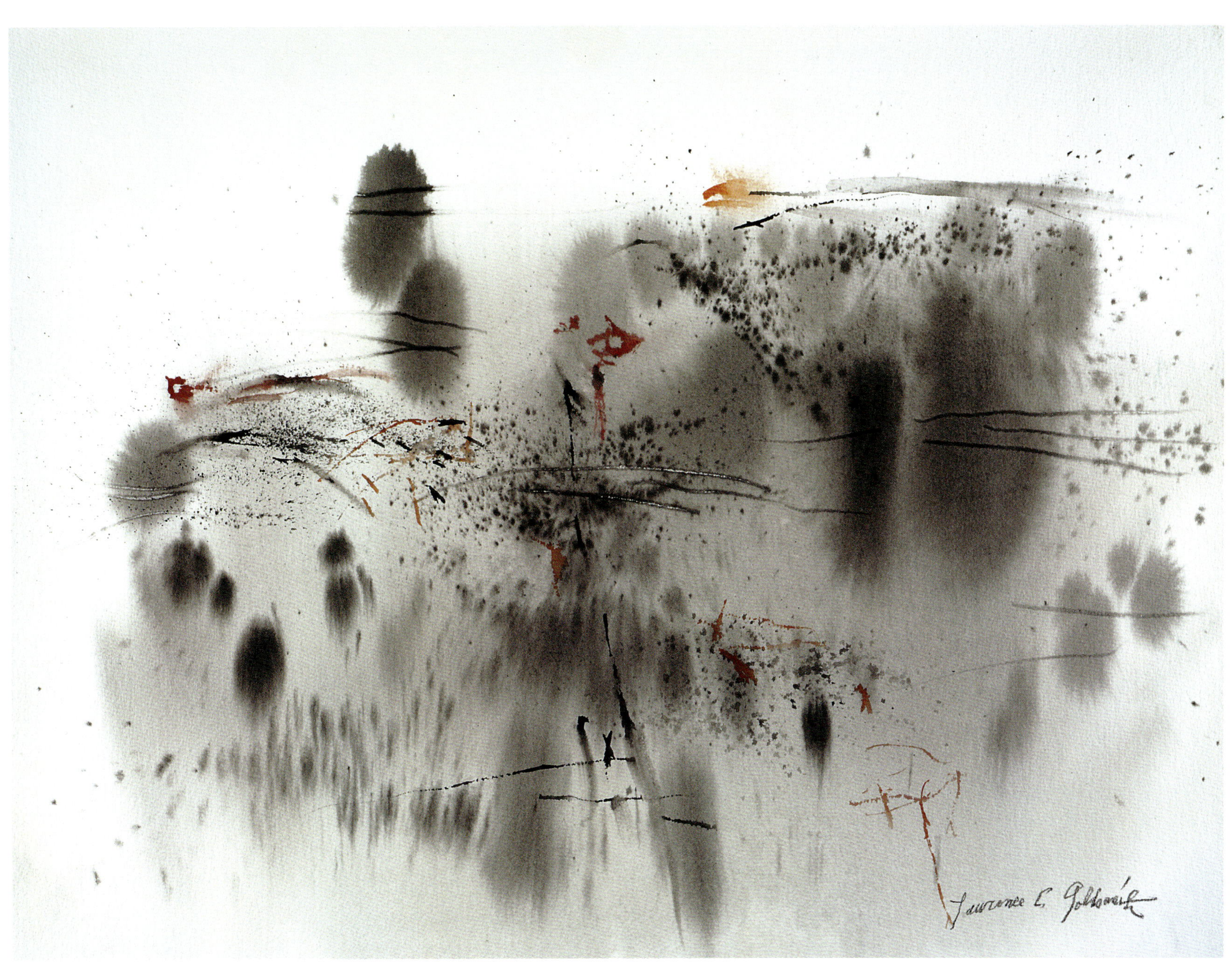

57 *Gray Vista*, 1998. A variety of grays can be as expressive as bright color. I add to this prospect by always making my own grays.

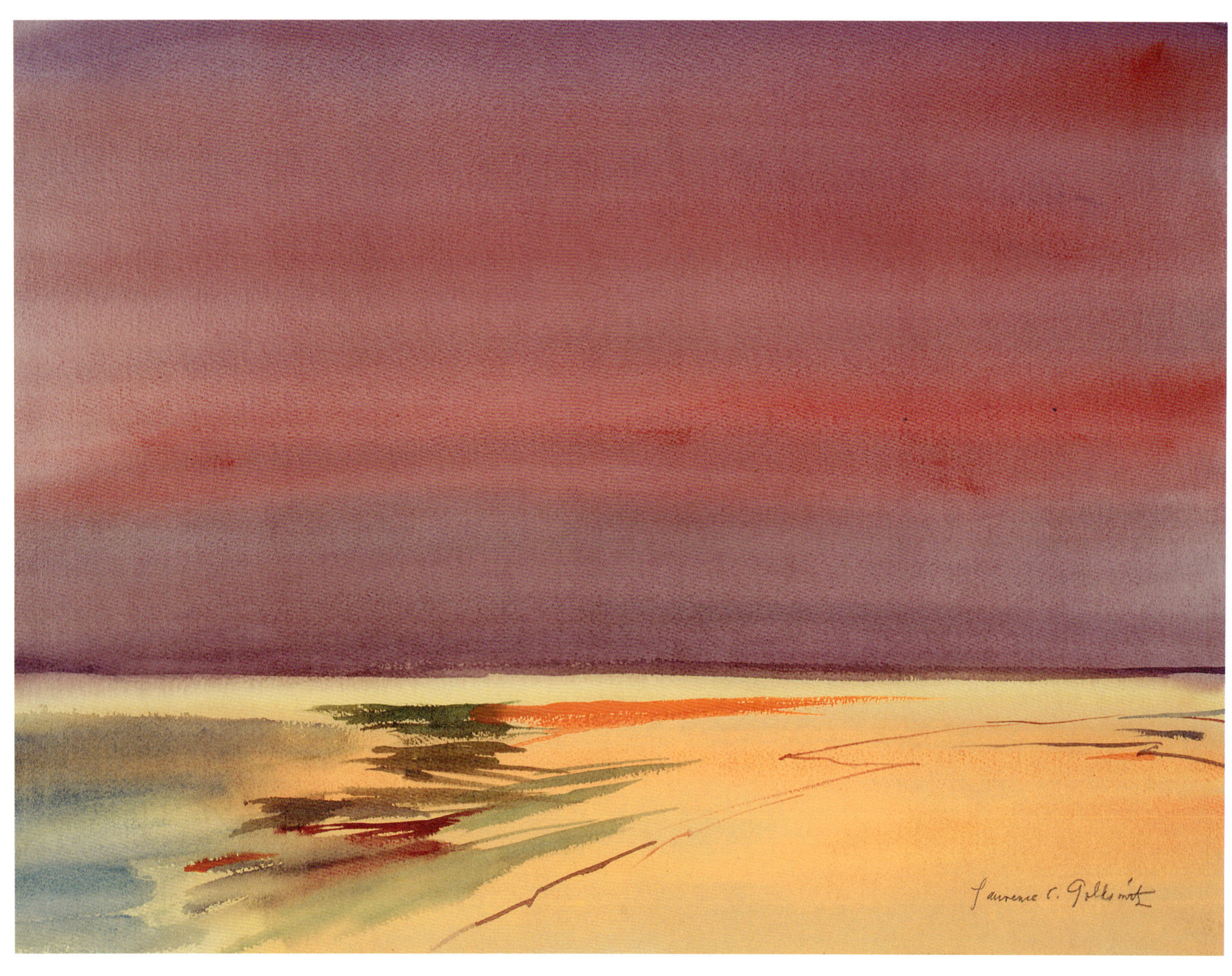

58 *Ruddy Cove,* 1998.

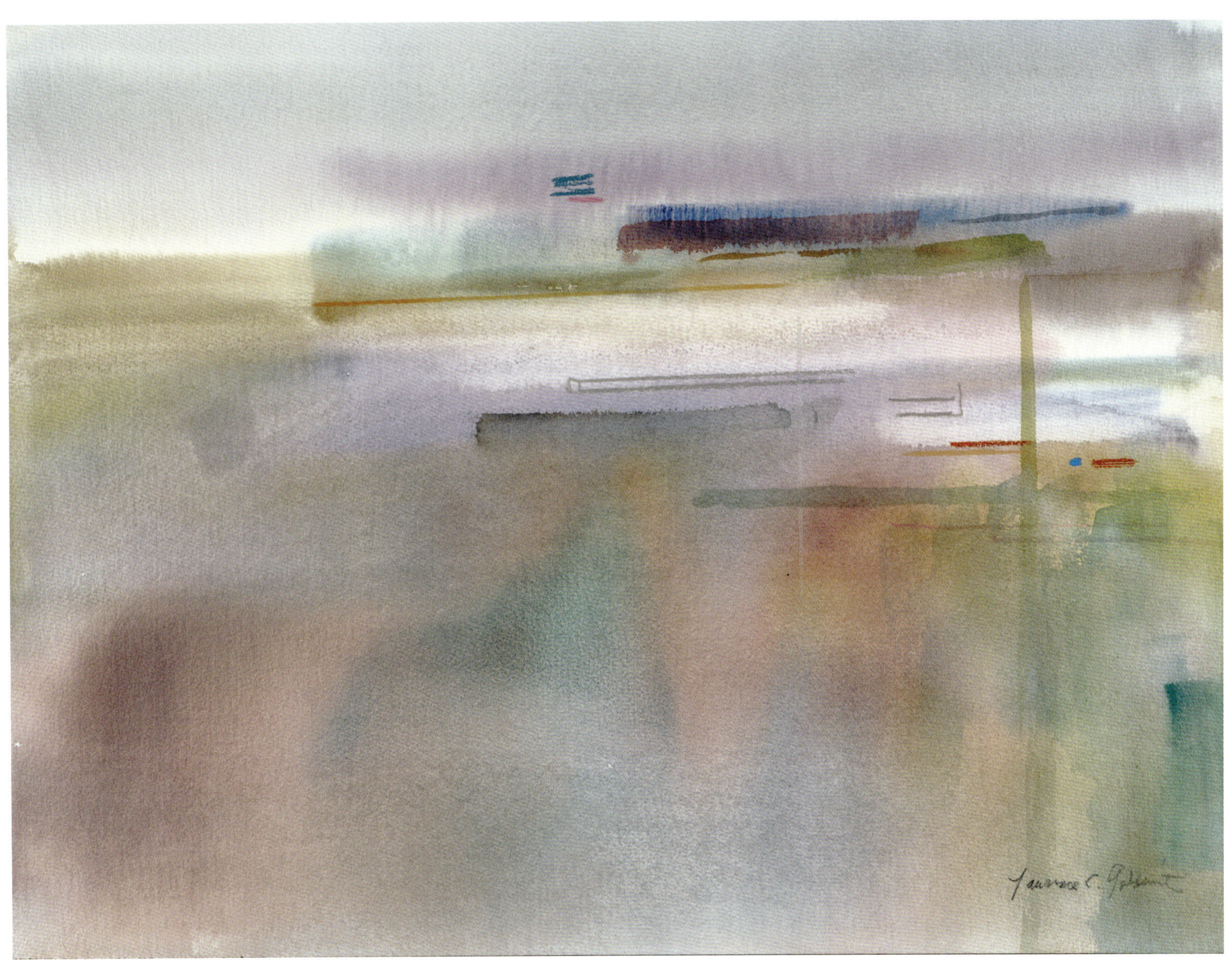

59 *Pocket Fog*, 1999. Private collection. For every visitor to the Maine Coast who deplores fog, there is another like me who enjoys its subtle conquest of the atmosphere.

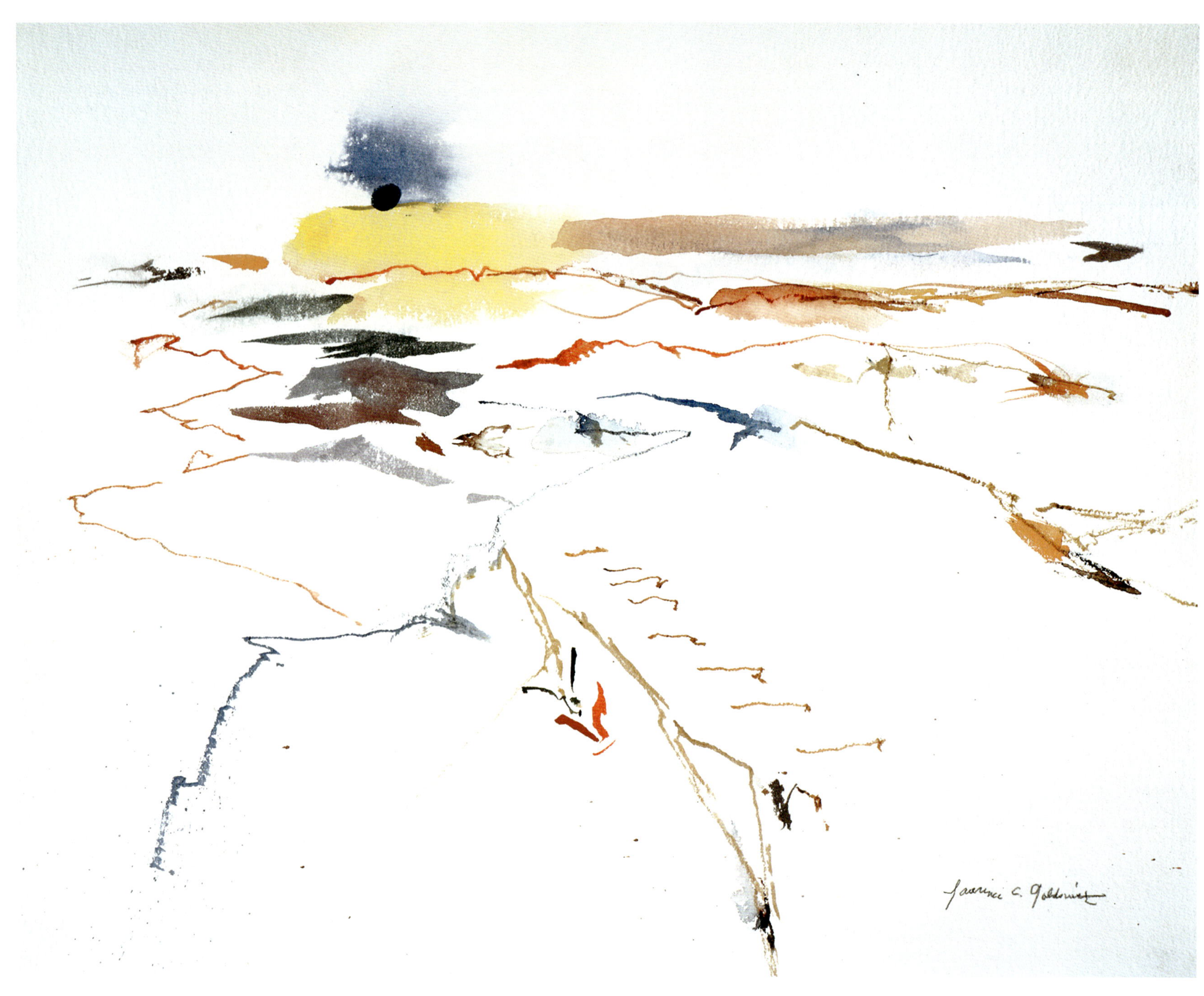

60 *Blue Spot*, 1999. 19 x 24 in. On Whatman paper, with a glittering white surface that lends itself beautifully to dry-brush work.

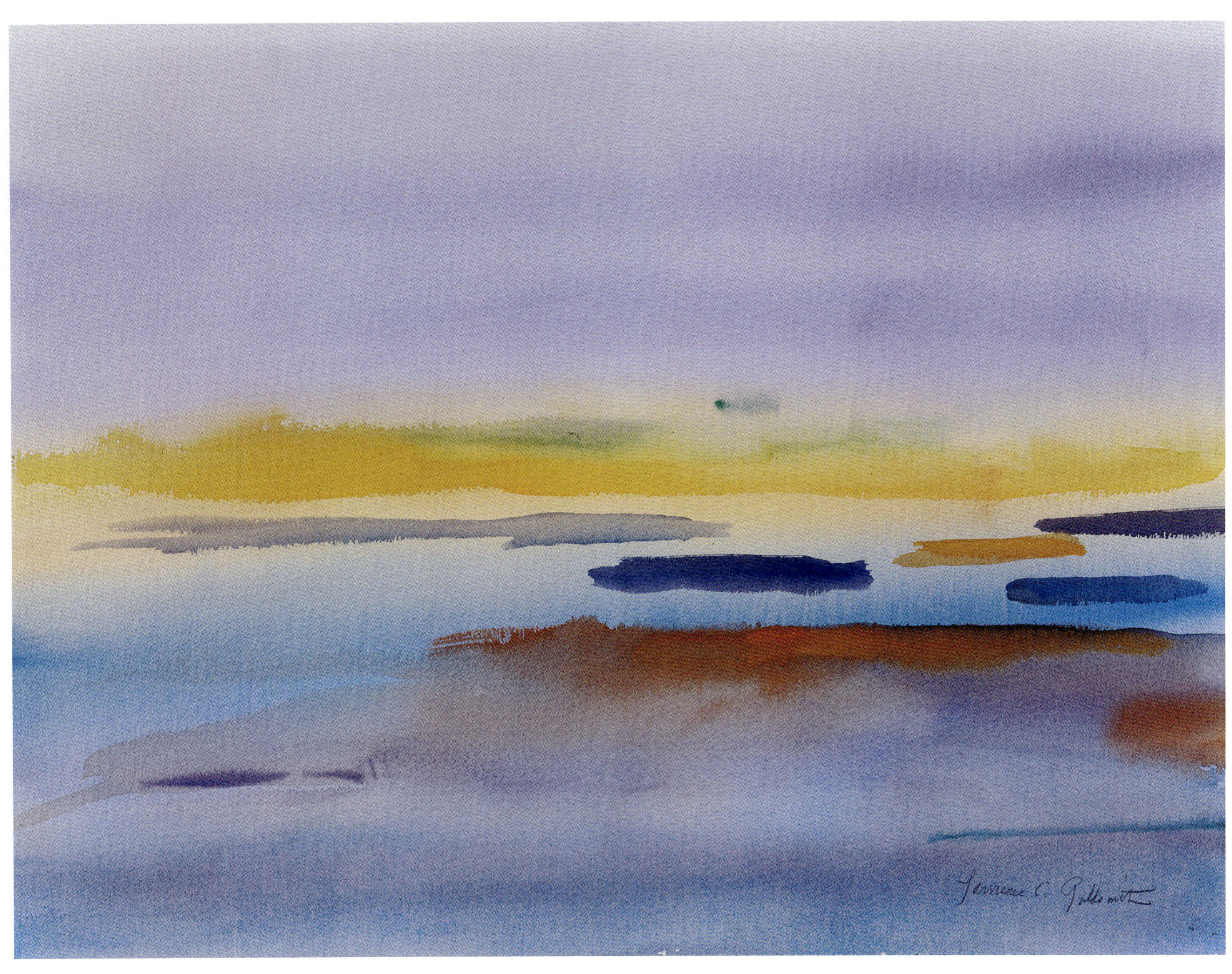

61 *Blue Sea*, 2001. My aim was to achieve the greatest simplification possible and still convey the mood. Another nod to Mark Rothko.

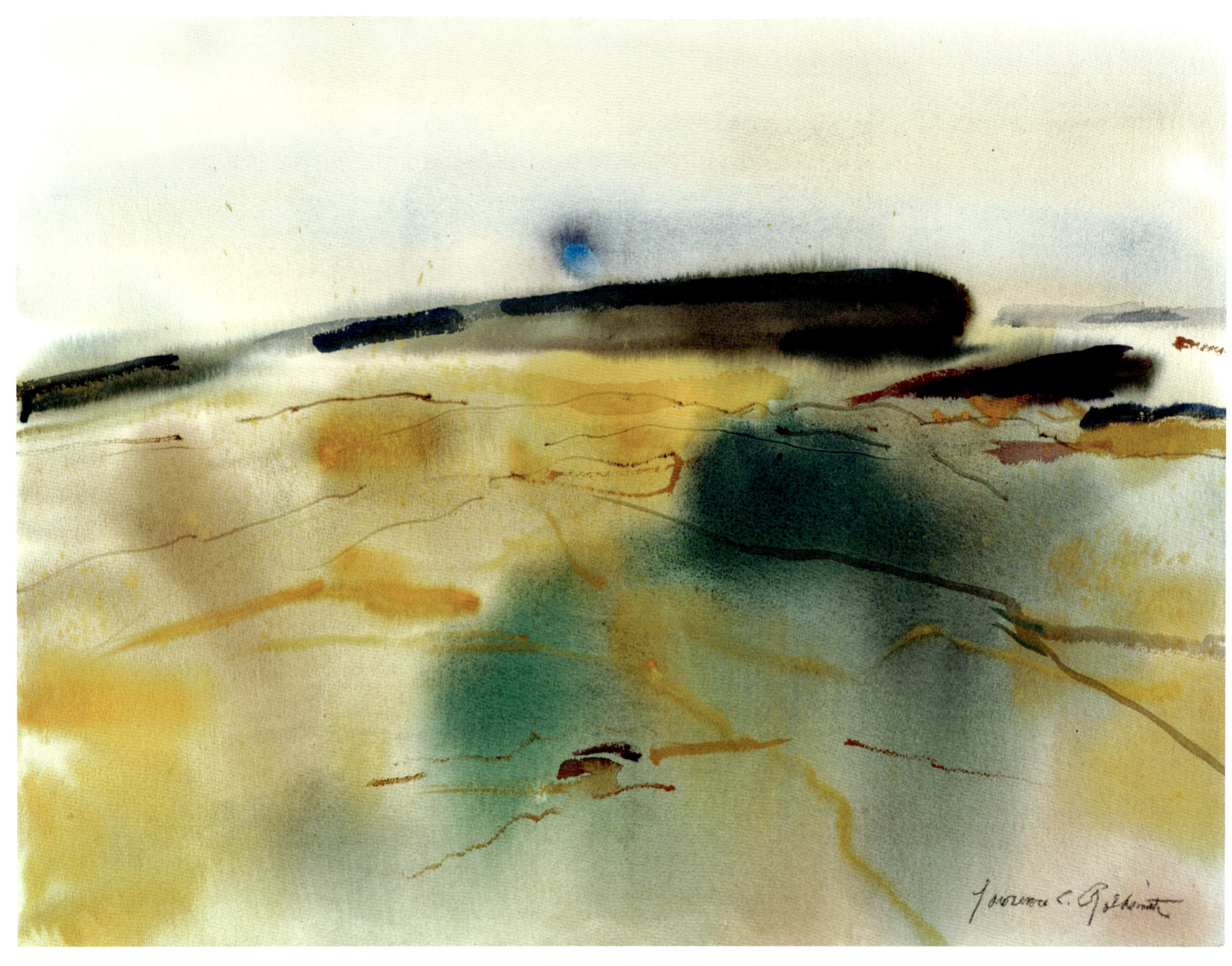

62 *Expectation,* 2001.

CHRONOLOGY

1916 Born November 22 in New York City.

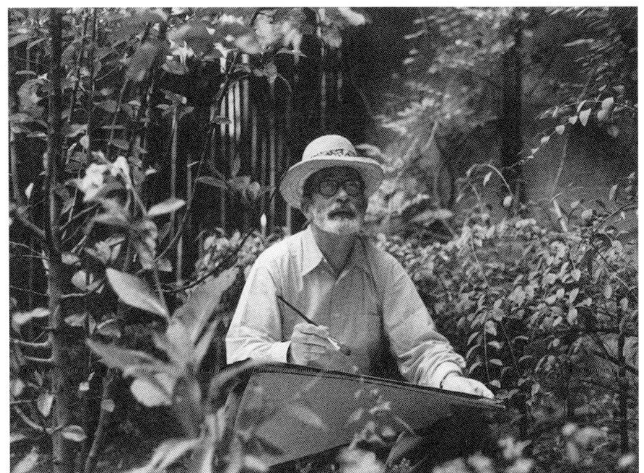

1965. In Greenwhich Village garden.

1922 Family moves to Scarsdale, NY, from Washington Heights.

1927–1928 Attends Grand Central School of Art. Wins class drawing prize.

1934–1939 Attends Yale University. Wins election to staff of Yale *Daily News*. Audits classes at Yale School of Fine Arts.

1939 Attends Eliot O'Hara watercolor workshop in New Haven, CT.

1942–1946 After being classified 4F, works for Office of War Information writing overseas radio broadcasts for Voice of America.

1943 Marries Victoria Hughes.

1944–1963 While working at various editorial jobs including the *New York Herald Tribune Sunday Magazine*, *Why* Magazine, *Family Circle*, and *Medical Economics*, freelances as oil painter and watercolorist. Takes courses in art history with Meyer Shapiro at the New School for Social Research, and in painting with Philip Evergood and Will Barnet, among others.

1945 Son Paul is born.

1946 Buys house in Fairfax, Vermont.

1952 Is divorced from wife Vicky.

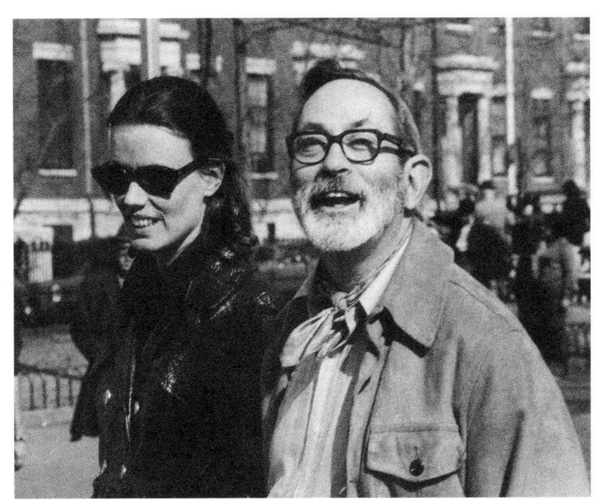

1971. In Greenwhich Village with Lynda.

1963–1971 Studies watercolor with Mario Cooper at the Art Students League.

1964 First visits Monhegan Island.

1964–1971 Studies painting with Reuben Tam at the Brooklyn Museum Art School.

1968 Is elected to membership in American Watercolor Society.

1968–1969 Works at Watson-Guptill art publishers, his last editorial job.

1970 Wins Winsor Newton award at National Arts Club watercolor show.

1969–1971 Teaches watercolor at Queens College, School of General Studies.

1970 Spends first full summer on Monhegan.

1971–1972 Teaches watercolor at Jackson Heights Art Club.

1972 Marries Lynda Strauss.

1973 Moves to Vermont.

1974–1993 Teaches courses and workshops first at Bellows Free Academy, Fairfax, then at University of Vermont's Church Street Center.

1978 Takes round-the-world trip with extended stays in Indonesia and Sri Lanka.

1980 *Watercolor Bold and Free* is published.

1983 With Lynda, buys house on Monhegan.

1988–1996 Six paintings are published as posters by Image Conscious of San Francisco.

2000 Paperback edition of *Watercolor Bold and Free* is released.

2003 Wins Award of Excellence at Art in the Round Barn show in Waitsfield, VT.

2004 Died at home in Vermont, March 7, age 87.

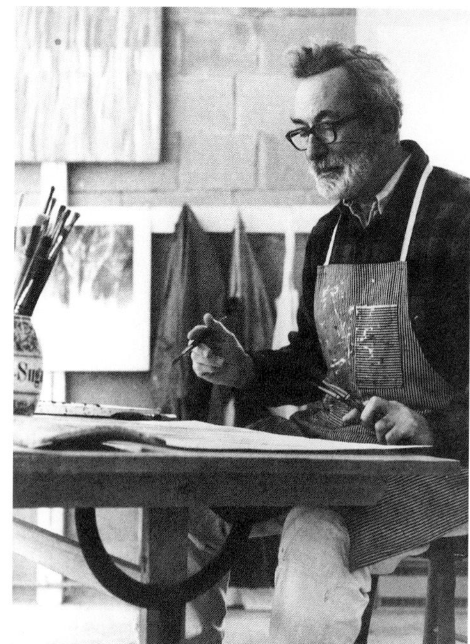

1973. In the new studio. Vermont.

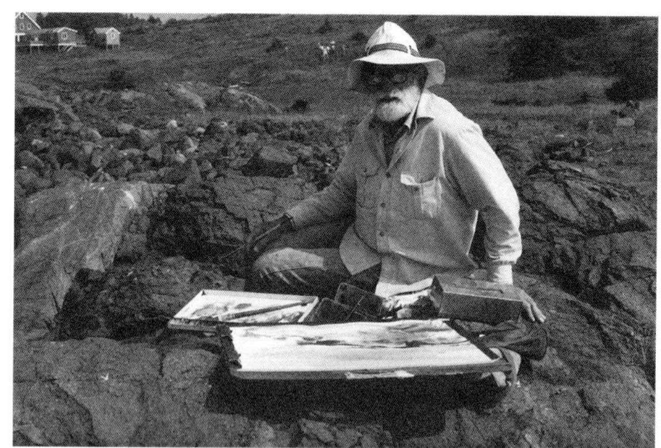

1987. Lobster Cove, Monhegan.

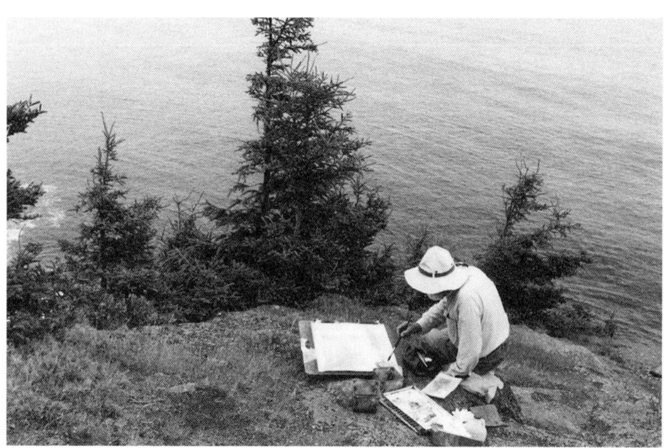

1990. Burnt Head, Monhegan.

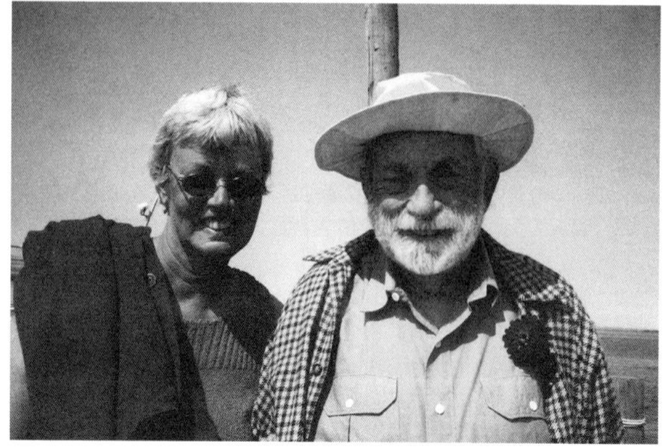

2003. Leaving Monhegan at summer's end, with Lynda.

COLLECTIONS

Brandstater Gallery, Loma Linda University, Riverside, CA

Currier Art Gallery, Manchester, NH

Danforth Museum, Framingham, MA

Farnsworth Museum, Rockland, ME

Fitchburg State College, Fitchburg, MA

Framingham State College, Framingham, MA

Lamont Gallery, Phillips Exeter Academy, Exeter, NH

Monhegan Museum, Monhegan, ME

Ogunquit Museum of American Art, Ogunquit, ME

Olin Arts Center, Bates College Museum of Art, Lewiston, ME

Robert Hull Fleming Museum, University of Vermont, Burlington, VT

Springfield Art Museum, Springfield, MO

University of Maine, Orono, ME

Yale University Art Gallery, New Haven, CT

EXHIBITIONS

SOLO EXHIBITIONS

1994 Pennino's Gallery, Burlington, VT
1993 Beside Myself Gallery, Arlington, VT
1987 Collectors Gallery, Shelburne, VT
1986 AVA Gallery, Hanover, NH
1985 Brandstater Gallery, Loma Linda University, Riverside, CA
1983 Church Street Center, University of Vermont, Burlington, VT
1983 South Huntington Public Library, South Huntington, NY
1982 State Office Building, Wilmington, DE
1982 The Gallery in the Square, Henniker, NH
1980 University of Maine at Orono, Orono, ME
1980 St. Paul's Cathedral, Burlington, VT
1979 Philadelphia Art Alliance, Philadelphia, PA
1977 Library Arts Center, Newport, NH
1977 Colby-Sawyer College, New London, NH
1976 Wood Gallery, Montpelier, VT
1975 Dibden Center, Johnson State College, Johnson, VT
1974 Rehoboth Art League, Rehoboth Beach, DE
1973 Gate House Studio, Manalapan, FL
1972 Lamont Gallery, Phillips Exeter Academy, Exeter, NH
1971 Caravan House, New York, NY
1966 Panoras Gallery, New York, NY
1964 Panoras Gallery, New York, NY

GROUP EXHIBITIONS

2003 Emerson Gallery, Hamilton College, Clinton, NY
Monhegan Artists: A 150-Year Tradition

2003 (also 1991–1997, 2001, 2002) Green Mountain Cultural Center, Waitsfield, VT
Art in the Round Barn annual exhibition

2002 Lore Degenstein Gallery, Susquehanna University, Selinsgrove, PA
Monhegan Modernists 1940–1970

2002 St. Paul's Cathedral, Burlington, VT

2001 (also 1988) Shelburne Farms, Shelburne, VT
Envisioned in a Pastoral Setting annual exhibition

2001 Olin Arts Center, Bates College, Lewiston, ME
Monhegan Paintings from the Collection of John Day

1999 Watercolor Art Society–Houston, Houston, TX

1999 Stratton Arts Festival, Stratton, VT

1998 Governor's Mansion, Augusta, ME
Monhegan Artists

1988 Bradford College, Bradford, MA

1988 (also 1986-1987) Marden Fine Arts, New York, NY

1987 South Huntington Public Library, South Huntington, NY

1986 Chaffee Art Center, Rutland, VT

1985 Helen Day Art Center, Stowe, VT

1985 San Diego Watercolor Society, San Diego, CA

1981 Champlain College, Burlington, VT

1981 AVA Gallery, Hanover, NH

1981 Georgia Watercolor Society, Columbus, GA

1981 Bette Cooper Gallery, Martha's Vineyard, MA

1981 Colbert Gallery, Montreal, Canada

1980–1981 Old Bergen Art Guild national tour:
Vermont Artists' Group

1980 Fresno Arts Center, Fresno, CA

1979 San Diego Watercolor Society, San Diego, CA

1979 (also 1976) Maine Coast Artists, Rockport, ME

1978 Church Street Center, University of Vermont, Burlington, VT

1978 La Galleria di Artisti Internazional, London, England

1977 Dartmouth College Hopkins Center, Hanover, NH

1976 Dartmouth College Hopkins Center, Hanover, NH

1974 Allentown Art Museum, Allentown, PA

1972 (also 1971, 1969, 1968, 1967) National Arts Club, New York, NY
Annual Watercolor Exhibition

1968 (also 1966, 1967) American Watercolor Society, New York, NY
Annual Exhibition

BIBLIOGRAPHY

Writings by Lawrence C. Goldsmith

"Friskt og freidig." *Kunst for Alle* (Oslo, 5 August 1997), 45–47. In Norwegian.

"The Watercolor Page." *American Artist* 39, no. 396 (July 1975), 42–45.

Watercolor Bold and Free. (New York: Watson-Guptill, 1980; paperbound edition 2000.)

"Watercolor Bold and Free." North Light 13, no. 2 (1981), 8–11. Excerpts from the book.

Articles about the artist

Ranson, Ron. "Three Steps to Heaven." *International Artist* 2, no. 7 (June/July 1999). 44–51.

Van Gelder, Pat. "A 'Zen Master of Watercolor'." *Watercolor* 2, no. 7 (Summer 1996). 118–123.

Who's Who in American Art.

Woolwich, Madlyn-Ann C. "Capturing the Spirit of a Landscape." *The Artist's Magazine* 13, no. 9 (September 1996), 78–80.

Books and articles referencing Goldsmith's work

Agar, Eunice. "Monhegan—An Artist's Island." *American Artist* 51, no. 538 (May, 1987), 49.

———. *Draw it! Paint it!* 2, part 23 (London: Watson-Guptill/Eaglemoss Publications, 1985), 626–627.

Betts, Edward. *Creative Seascape Painting,* 133. (New York: Watson-Guptill, 1981.)

Blake, Wendon. *Acrylic Watercolor Painting,* 69. (New York: Watson-Guptill, 1970.)

Blake, Wendon. *Complete Guide to Acrylic Painting,* 47. (New York: Watson-Guptill, 1971.)

Compton, Annette. *Drawing from the Mind, Painting from the Heart: 12 Essential Lessons to Becoming a Better Artist.* (New York: Watson-Guptill, 2002.)

Curtis, Jane and Will, and Frank Lieberman, *Monhegan: The Artists' Island,* 128. (Camden, ME: Down East Books, 1995.)

Day, John M. "Monhegan: The Abstracted Island." *American Art Review* 13, no. 4 (July–August 2001), 174–181.

Doherty, M. Stephen, "Recent Images, Recent Concerns." Watercolor 92: 42–43. (New York: *American Artist* Magazine, 1992.)

Grunebaum, James. *Friendship: Liberty, Equality, and Utility.* (Albany: SUNY Press, 2003.) Cover.

Leland, Nita. *Exploring Color,* 114, 171. (Cincinnati: North Light Publishers, 1998.)

Meyer, Susan E. 40 *Watercolorists and How They Work,* 34–37. (New York: Watson-Guptill, 1976.)

Ranson, Ron. *Distilling the Scene,* 120–121. (Newton Abbot, Great Britain: David & Charles, 1994.)

Thomashow, Mitchell. *Bringing the Biosphere Home: Learning to Perceive Global Environmental Change.* (Cambridge, MA: MIT Press, 2001.) Jacket.

Thomashow, Mitchell. *Ecological Identity: Becoming a Reflective Environmentalist.* (Cambridge, MA: MIT Press, 1995.) Jacket.

INDEX